9 to 19

CRUCIAL YEARS
FOR SELF-ESTEEM
IN CHILDREN & YOUTH

James Battle, PhD

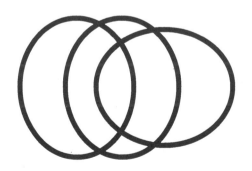

James Battle and Associates
#406, Edwards Building
10053 - 111 Street
Edmonton, Alberta T5K 2H8

International Standard Book Number: 09694352-0-7

Canadian Cataloguing in Publication Data II. Title
BF697.5S46B38 1990 649'.125 C90-090049-0

Sixth Reprint 1994

CONTENTS

Many people have contributed to the development and publication of this book. First, I recognize and thank the hundreds of parents who participated in the seminars, workshops, and parenting courses that provided the major impetus which resulted in the development of this book. Second, I thank the many, many parents who permitted me to interact with their children in our combined attempts to assist children in achieving their potential effectively. Third, I thank Ms. Liz O'Neill (executive director) and the board of directors of the Big Sister Society of Edmonton for their sponsorship of many of the workshops and seminars for parents and volunteers. Fourth, I gratefully acknowledge the many children and adults who participated in the studies that are cited in this book. Fifth, I thank my wife Dorothy and her mother Edith Cary for typing the manuscript. Finally, I dedicate this book to parents everywhere who are striving to enhance the self-esteem and development of their children.

James Battle

PREFACE

I have served as a school and counseling psychologist for parents and their children for nearly twenty years, and during this period it has become apparent to me that self-esteem is the most important variable affecting a child's ability to develop his or her potential effectively. Thus, it seems reasonable to assume that the most effective way of promoting the development of children is to help parents to understand the important effects that self-esteem—high and low—have on children's behavior, and to provide practical information which can help parents become more effective.

Parenting is a complex process that is becoming progressively more demanding. The pressures created by our rapidly changing contemporary society heavily tax the coping strategies of both parent and child. Effective strategies that can be applied in day-to-day interactions can benefit parents, children, and society. To provide these is the goal of this book.

This book is unique in a number of ways. First, it is among the first to provide practical suggestions for parents, teachers, and other caretakers, to assist them in their attempts to enhance the self-esteem of the children they have in their charge. Second, it provides an overview of the issue of self-esteem in a style and with vocabulary that is appropriate for the lay audience and professionals as well.

This book is organized into four parts:

Part I provides an introduction to the study of important variables of self-esteem. It also provides a brief overview of the school of phenomenology and defines the construct of self-esteem. Characteristics of self-esteem are delineated, and its development is documented.

Part II describes the role that self-esteem plays in the adjustment process. We will describe the consequences of disordered self-esteem and review the pathological conditions of childhood depression and childhood suicide. In addition, strategies for remediating disordered self-esteem are described.

Part III sketches the important process of enhancement of self-esteem. Motives that compel children's behavior are described, and specific strategies for enhancing children's self-esteem are discussed in detail.

Part IV provides an annotated list of recommended readings and references to the book.

I

SELF-ESTEEM: AN OVERVIEW

INTRODUCTION

Self-esteem is a fundamental human need. All people strive to develop and maintain self-esteem. Those who do not develop an adequate sense of self-esteem attempt to "fake it," using defensive mechanisms to display what Branden (1969) calls "inauthentic self-esteem."

Parents are the most significant people affecting the self-esteem of their children; therefore, how parents interact with their children exerts a major effect on their children's self-esteem. This book is an attempt to assist parents in interacting more effectively with their children, which will have a positive effect on their children's self-esteem and which, in turn, will enable their offspring fully to develop their potential. Since teachers, psychologists, psychiatrists, social workers, and other caretakers are likewise influences on children, this book also offers suggestions and strategies that professionals can use in their work with children.

In writing this book I made a concerted effort to provide a text that would offer a balance between scholarship and interest which will satisfy both the curiosity of the professional and the day-to-day needs of the parent. I emphasize the importance of the interactive process and delineate practical procedures that parents and helping professionals can use in their attempts to assist children.

Self-esteem is a prominent and persistent need that encompasses one's entire existence. Self-esteem affects one's mental health, achievement patterns, and relationships with others. The need of self-esteem has become of central importance to all of us because the pressures associated with our rapidly changing society have created a high degree of stress—stress that is harmful to children and youth. Societal pressures have resulted in problems we have heard about often: alienation, depression, and delinquency. For instance, depression in children—which is generally associated with low self-esteem (Battle 1978, 1980; Paananen 1983)—has increased significantly during the last decade; and suicide, which typically follows depression, is among the leading causes of death of North American youth ages 9 to 19.

Although many of the problems experienced by today's parents are similar to those of their predecessors, some are unique, and therefore require innovative forms of intervention. A book of this nature, which provides practical suggestions for parents and caretakers of children, is thus timely. We can do no less: Children are worthy of our efforts because they are our most valuable resource.

Chapter 1

UNDERSTANDING BEHAVIOR:
A PHENOMENOLOGICAL POINT OF VIEW

There are many theoretical views that attempt to explain human behavior. In this book, we emphasize the phenomenological view because its tenets allow consideration of the importance of self-esteem. The school of phenomenology is that group of psychologists who assume that subjective perception is the major determinant of human behavior. Phenomenologists have made the most significant contributions to the study of the self and generally propose that each individual reacts to the world in terms of his or her unique perception of it. As these theorists reason, perception—not objective reality—determines one's behavior in every instance. Accordingly, our subjective perception of self-worth (self-esteem) determines our characteristic reactions. "Reality" does not exist in the event, but rather in the phenomenon . . . that is, the individual's experience of the event. If a child's perceptions are distorted to the extent that they are grossly incongruent with reality, these perceptions in every instance determine the child's behavior. If a child is quite capable, but perceives that he or she possesses little potential, that child will function in a fashion that is consistent with the perception: The capable child who is self-demeaning is as counterproductive, as self-defeating, as the less capable or poorly equipped child who is self-demeaning to the same extent. Support for this position is provided by Rogers (1959), as well as by our own earlier studies (Battle 1982, p. 19). The issue of perceived reality is important on all levels, including the physical: If an infant is held by a friendly, affectionate person, but perceives this experience as being strange and frightening, the child will consequently react or respond to this experience by displaying fear. The following case (Battle 1982, pp. 13-14) illustrates the role that perception plays in behavior.

Case Report 1:1. Bob.

Bob was an average seventeen-year-old senior attending a small midwestern high school. Near the end of his senior year, Bob and other graduating seniors journeyed to the university to take college entrance examinations. Bob earned an average score on his examination, but a computer error assigned him a score at the 95th percentile. When Bob's test results reached the school, his principal was shocked to discover that Bob had earned the highest score in his school and was among the top 2 percent in the entire state. He found this particularly difficult to accept, because he and other faculty had always viewed Bob as being an average student. The principal, nevertheless, reassessed his perceptions of Bob and started to view him as being a very capable student. When the results were viewed by the counselor, he reassessed his perceptions of Bob, and assumed that the average standardized test scores Bob had earned throughout the years, apparently, were not valid indicators of his true level of potential. When Bob's results were observed by his home-room teacher, she reassessed her views of Bob. When she informed Bob's parents of his score, they started to view him differently.

After observing the way his principal, counselor, teacher, and parents were reacting toward him, Bob reassessed his perceptions of himself and started to see himself as not merely being "average" but quite capable. Subsequently, Bob became one of the highest achievers of his era. He is now a practicing physician.

Perception in most cases (as in the case of Bob) determines whether or not the individual makes significant or routine contributions to society, because how we view ourselves determines how we respond to the demands of the environment.

Behavior

We support the view which proposes that all human behavior has purpose and is goal-directed. We recognize that an individual may not be aware of the motives compelling his or her behavior; but we nevertheless feel that in every instance behavior is guided or directed by some underlying purpose. This position is vividly illustrated by Adler (1927, p. 29) in the following passage:

> Psychic life of man is determined by his goal. No human being can think, feel, will, dream, without all these activities being determined, continued, modified, and directed toward an ever-present objective . . . . A real understanding of the behavior of any human being is impossible without a clear comprehension of the secret goal which he is pursuing.

Birth Order and Behavior

The idea that birth order influences behavior is not a new one. It dates back to Galton (1874), who proposed that birth order was an important factor affecting the contributions of English scientists (Miley 1969, p. 64). More recent theorists (most notably Adler, 1927) believe that one's ordinal position in the family exerts a strong effect on one's perception of self-worth and behavior. Adler communicated his emphasis on the importance of birth order when he said:

> Above all, we must rid ourselves of the superstition that the situation within the family is the same for each individual child.

Adler thought that, although siblings live in the same home setting, they do not experience identical social environments because they are not treated in exactly the same fashion by parents and significant others. The first born, for instance, typically receives a tremendous amount of parental attention until the second child comes along. When the second child is born, the oldest feels "dethroned," and as a consequence typically starts to misbehave in an attempt to recapture his former position as the center of attention of parents. The first born, however, cannot succeed, because the younger child needs considerable attention. As a result of this inevitable "dethroning" experience, the oldest child is often oriented toward the past, pessimistic about the future, and prone to develop emotional problems. In addition, the oldest child tends to be conscientious, conservative, responsible, and compliant.

The second born is typically a more secure child because he or she does not experience the traumatic "dethronement" that the first born must endure. Resulting from his ordinal position, the second born often experiences pressure from both sides (from the oldest and from the youngest), and as a consequence frequently develops highly competitive modes of behaving—which often enable him to develop at a faster rate than the first born child. It is often observed that second born children tend to speak at an earlier age than first borns. Adler felt that the second born child was the one most likely to develop favorably.

The youngest child is typically an ambitious, high achieving individual who generally attempts to surpass older siblings. If the youngest child is spoiled or pampered, however, he or she frequently displays inadequacy and assumes that others should take care of personal needs. Because parents tend to spoil the youngest child, these children may experience difficulties due to an unwillingness to work up to potential. The youngest child frequently behaves like a helpless individual who is incapable of doing things independently.

In families in which there are more than three children, proponents of Adlerian psychology generally agree that children will display variable behavior. For instance, the third child in a family of four children would probably behave like a middle child, whereas the second child in a family of this size may display the type of behavior one would otherwise expect of the oldest child.

The only child is of course the first born; but unlike the oldest child, this child does not experience "dethronement" and loss of prominence. The only child is the focus of parents' attention—and, as a consequence of this attention, often matures earlier than is typical of first born children. This attention can have negative affects on the only child's development because he runs the risk of overvaluing personal worth and having unrealistic expectations regarding the amount of attention he should receive. When the only child enters school, for instance, he often finds it difficult to understand why he cannot be the center of the teacher's attention. The only child's egocentricity often results in behavioral problems and strained relationships with other pupils—frequently resulting in ostracism by peers. Adler felt that only children tend to be timid and dependent, and generally possess lower-than-average social interest because they find it difficult to concern themselves with the needs of others.

Other writers (e.g., Coopersmith 1967; Rosenberg 1965; Schultz 1983) also propose that birth order is related to self-esteem. Coopersmith found that first born and only children earned higher self-esteem scores, and Rosenberg found that only children earned higher self-esteem scores, than average. Schultz studied 542 fifth-grade students and found a significant relationship between birth order and social self-esteem as measured by the *Culture-Free Self-Esteem Inventory for Children* (Battle 1981), with the relationship being the strongest for middle children.

Although some experts, such as Adler, assume that birth order is a major variable affecting behavior, we think that perception is *the* most important variable affecting behavior. These positions are not so contradictory as they may seem, however. How parents interact with their children in light of ordinal birth position affects the child's perception of self-worth, which in turn determines his or her characteristic mode of behaving.

Understanding Misbehavior

Although children, and teenagers too, prefer to obtain their purposes by cooperating or behaving "appropriately," some feel compelled to manifest misbehavior, which generally impedes self-esteem and parents' attempts to assist their children in developing their potential. Misbehavior, like behavior in general, has purpose and goals. Keeping in mind that the person may not be aware of the purpose or goal, we see children display misbehavior when their interactions with people significant to them are negative and when they are discouraged.

The most commonly quoted goals of children's misbehavior are those noted by Dreikurs (1971). Dreikurs enumerated the four goals of children's misbehavior: (1) attention, (2) power, (3) revenge, and (4) display of inadequacy.

Attention. The desire for attention is almost universal in children. Children prefer to obtain attention by behaving in a cooperative, positive fashion; however, if they cannot get the attention they desire by behaving positively, they will emit negative behavior in these attempts. For example, if a child with a learning disability cannot get the teacher's attention by performing well academically, he or she may seek attention by misbehavior. Thus, children experiencing learning disabilities often develop behavior problems. For another example, when a child refuses to go to bed, she is generally wanting attention. When she annoys her parents by insisting on a snack, then a drink of water, and—after these—permission to use the bathroom, attention is the sought-for goal.

Power. When the child's goal of misbehavior is power, he generally attempts to demonstrate to parents and other adults that they can't make him do anything that he doesn't want to do. Children seeking power feel that they are significant only when they are "the boss"; therefore, they may refuse to cooperate and frequently involve themselves in power struggles in their interactions with peers, parents, and other adults (e.g., teachers). The child displaying a bid for power may be overtly defiant in his interactions with others or resist passively. The latter, covert negativism, can be conveyed subtly. when the child *appears* to be compliant, but nonetheless refuses to do what adults want him to do. Any teacher or parent who has heard, "I'll do it in a minute," only to find the requested task never performed, has experienced a child wielding power.

Revenge. Children who pursue revenge are hurt; as a consequence, they want to hurt others. Children who are seeking revenge feel that they have been mistreated by those important to them (e.g., parents), and strive to "get even" with those they feel are responsible for the mistreatment. In their attempts to retaliate, for example, many of such children underachieve; if achievement is an important goal of parents for their children, this is an effective way of disappointing those expectations. Similarly, adolescents who are seeking revenge often act their feelings out sexually and get deeply involved in drugs in order to hurt parents they feel have mistreated them.

The following case of Kathy is offered to illustrate how adolescents pursuing revenge often behave.

Case Report 1:2. Kathy; 15 years, 8 months.

Kathy, who was adopted when she was two months old, was the youngest child in a family with three children. Kathy's early development was generally normal. She walked at 10 months, started to use sentences at 17 months, and was toilet trained at 2 years, 4 months.

Kathy entered kindergarten at age four and a half and first grade when she was five. Kathy was a "model" student during the elementary school years—an honor student who was placed in a "gifted" class when she was in fifth grade. Her behavior was generally positive until her teen years. Kathy's problems began to manifest themselves when she was 12 and in the eighth grade.

Kathy reported, "When I turned 12, I started to hate my stepfather"; but she didn't provide an explanation for this sudden onset of dislike for him. Until this point, she had been her dad's favorite daughter, and they had generally enjoyed a very positive relationship. At this time of onset, Kathy's relationship with her stepmother was more positive than with her stepfather; but they experienced difficulties because Kathy felt her mother was an unaffectionate person who was too strict and punitive. During the eighth-grade year Kathy started to use drugs, underachieve, and have sexual intercourse with numerous boys. She got into fights on several occasions at school; and, as a consequence of her misbehavior, she was subsequently placed in a private school when she was 13. Her behavior was so deviant in this setting that she was expelled two years later. At age 15 Kathy's stepmother referred her to a psychologist for assessment and treatment. The psychologist found Kathy to be a very bright youngster. Her Verbal, Performance, and Full Scale IQ scores on the *Wechsler Intelligence Scale for Children* were 115, 135, and 128 respectively. The psychologist diagnosed Kathy as being an adolescent who was experiencing a "conduct disorder, undersocialized aggressive type," and provided her with psychotherapy. According to the psychologist, the goal of Kathy's misbehavior was revenge intended to hurt parents who she felt put conditions on their love for her and who set unrealistically high expectations for her that were—in her view—unattainable. Although some gains were made during psychotherapy, she continued to misbehave. Because of her persistent misbehavior, Kathy was placed in a group home for juvenile delinquents.

Display of Inadequacy. Children who display inadequacy or disability attempt to convince others that they *can't* do things. They often present themselves as being dumb, incapable, hopeless. These maneuvers, however, are manipulative and are representative of the child's attempt to get others to do things for him or her.

The following case of Tommy provides a typical illustration of a child displaying inadequacy.

Case Report 1:3. Tommy; 12 years, 5 months.

Tommy was the youngest child, the only boy in a family of four children. His parents were middle-aged, and he was ten years younger than his sister closest in age to him. Tommy's development during his first six years was within normal limits. He walked at 12 months, started using sentences at 20 months, and was toilet trained at 2 years, 10 months.

Tommy was enrolled in kindergarten at the age of four and a half. Kindergarten was a good year for Tommy, and he functioned quite well in first and second grade. He started to experience academic difficulties in third grade, however, and continued to experience problems throughout the elementary years and grades seven and eight. Because of Tommy's persistent academic problems, his parents joined the local chapter of parents of children with learning disabilities because they assumed that he "had a learning disability." Tommy's teachers generally reported that he was having difficulties in reading and spelling, but that he enjoyed arithmetic and performed fairly well in that area. His teachers also generally reported that they felt Tommy could earn better grades; and his fifth- and sixth-grade teachers recommended that he repeat; but his parents refused to let him repeat because they felt repeating would exert a negative effect on his self-esteem.

When Tommy was failing eighth grade, his parents referred him to a psychologist. The psychologist administered an IQ test to Tommy and found him to be a bright youngster with Verbal, Performance, and Full Scale IQ scores of 109, 115, and 113 respectively, on the *Wechsler Intelligence Scale for Children*. The psychologist diagnosed Tommy as an egocentric child who was underachieving and "displaying inadequacy." The psychologist recommended that Tommy's parents and teachers cooperate closely and ensure that he would make an "appropriate" effort before giving up on a task. They were told that, if he did not complete tasks that he was capable of completing during regularly scheduled periods, he should be required to do them during his free periods or at home after school.

After this recommended structure was implemented, Tommy made significant academic progress:

. . . .

Test	Grade Score June 1979	Grade Score February 1980	Grade Score August 1980
Schonell Reading	4.4	5.6	6.6
Schonell Spelling	3.5	5.2	5.5
Schonell Comp.	4.5	7.8	9.2
Bett's Vocab.	4.5	6.1	6.2
Monroe-Sherman	5.5	5.8	9.8

. . . .

Identifying Misbehavior

Parents and other adults can identify the goals of children's misbehavior by identifying how they feel when the children misbehave. Two popular contemporary psychologists, Dinkmeyer and McKay (1976), propose that parents and other adults tend to feel annoyed when the children's goal of misbehavior is attention; angry, when the child's goal is power; hurt, when the child's goal is revenge; and they feel like giving up in despair when the child's goal is a display of inadequacy.

SUMMARY

1. Self-esteem is a need that encompasses one's entire experience. Self-esteem affects one's mental health, achievement patterns, and interactions with others.
2. Phenomenologists hold the position that subjective perception is the major determinant of behavior, and that each individual reacts to the world in terms of his or her perception of it.
3. Behavior has purpose, and all of us are mostly influenced by social forces.
4. Birth order is an important factor influencing behavior because it affects one's perception of self-worth.
5. Children display misbehavior when their interactions with people significant to them are negative, and when they are discouraged.

Chapter 2

SELF-ESTEEM: WHAT IS IT?

Self-esteem is a topic that has received considerable attention recently; however, there still exists controversy regarding "what is self-esteem." Our first task, therefore, is to define self-esteem. In spite of the fact that there is no general
consensus on a universal definition, most experts assume
that self-esteem refers to the individual's perception of his
or her own worth. Experts also typically agree that subjective perception determines the way one behaves and that
an individual's actions, in turn, influence the way he perceives himself.

Self-Concept and Self-Esteem

Although some experts do not differentiate between
self-concept and self-esteem, I feel that distinctions should
be made. Self-concept and self-esteem are closely related;
but the two constructs, nevertheless, refer to different aspects of the self. Thus, we have the following differential
definitions.
Self-concept defined. Coopersmith (1967) defines the

self-concept as being:

... The totality of perceptions a person has about himself which are most vital to the individual himself and that seem to that individual to be "me" at all times and places.

Rogers (1951, p. 136) offers the following definition of self-concept:

The self-concept or self-structure may be thought of as an organized configuration of perceptions of the self which are admissable to awareness. It is composed of such elements as the perceptions of one's characteristics and abilities; the percepts and concepts of self in relation to others and to the environment; the value qualities which are perceived as associated with experiences and objects; and goals and ideals which are perceived as having positive or negative value.

Bryne (1974, p. 271) offers the following definition:

The self-concept may be defined simply as the total collection of attitudes, judgments, and values which an individual holds with respect to his behavior, his ability, his body, his worth as a person, in short, how he perceives and evaluates himself.

Muller and Leonetti (1974, p. 5) define the self-concept accordingly:

The self-concept is the self-description the individual provides of himself.

Although the definitions just listed differ slightly, their similarities outweigh observed differences. They all indicate that the self-concept is comprised of more than one dimension and that it possesses perceptual and evaluative components, as well.

Self-esteem defined. Coopersmith (1967) defines self-esteem as being.

... The evaluation which the individual makes and customarily maintains with regard to himself. It expresses an attitude of approval or disapproval and indicates the extent to which the individual believes himself to be capable, significant, successful, and worthy.

Branden (1969, p. 110), in his book *The Psychology of*

Self-Esteem, states that self-esteem refers to:

> . . . An individual's view of himself. Self-esteem has two interrelated aspects. It entails a sense of personal efficacy and a sense of personal worth. It is the integrated sum of self-confidence and self-respect. It is the conviction that one is competent to live and [is] worthy of living.

In another publication (1981, p. 14), I myself state:

> Self-esteem refers to the perception the individual possesses of his own worth. An individual's perception of self develops gradually and becomes more differentiated as he matures and interacts with significant others. Perception of self-worth, once established, tends to be fairly stable and resistant to change.

Although authorities disagree regarding a universal definition of self-esteem, they generally assume that it is: (1) a subjective evaluative phenomenon, (2) multifaceted, (3) stable, and (4) gradual in its development.

A subjective evaluative phenomenon. Self-esteem is viewed by most experts as being a disposition that the individual possesses pertaining to his own worth. This disposition, of course, is subjective; and the individual makes some evaluation regarding his or her own worth based on this disposition.

As the child matures, he learns to evaluate his performance in relation to others (e.g., parents, peers, academically, etc.) and in accordance with an ideal that is dictated by his superego. Take, for example, the case of the child who feels that he has to be flawless in order to be worthy of a positive self-evaluation. The individual who evaluates his performance with this standard would tend to perceive himself "negatively" if his performance were in any way less than perfect. Thus, a student may be earning B's, which satisfies his teacher and parents, but feels "dumb" because—personally—he feels he should earn A's (Battle 1982, p. 25).

Multifaceted. Self-esteem is not a unitarian phenomenon; rather, it is multifaceted. That is, it is comprised of a number of interrelated facets. Self-esteem, as measured by the *Culture-Free Self-Esteem Inventory for Children* (Battle 1981), includes general, social, academic, and parent dimensions.

The general dimension involves an overall or general view of one's perception of his own worth; the social dimension refers to the individual's perception of interpersonal peer relationships; the academic component refers to the individual's perception of his ability to succeed academically; the parental (home) dimension refers to the individual's perception of his status at home, which includes his subjective perception of how he feels his parents view him (Battle 1982, p. 23).

Typical items incorporated in the *Culture-Free Self-Esteem Inventory for Children* that assess the multifaceted dimensions of children's self-esteem are:

General self-esteem items:
- I am happy most of the time.
- I usually fail when I try to do important things.

Social self-esteem items:
- Boys and girls like to play with me.
- I can do things as well as other boys and girls.

Academic self-esteem items:
- Most boys and girls are smarter than I am.
- I am proud of my school work.

Parent-related self-esteem items:
- My parents make me feel that I am not good enough.
- My parents understand how I feel.

Items incorporated in the *Culture-Free Self-Esteem Inventory for Adults* (Battle 1981), which is suitable for most teenagers as well, assess these dimensions:

General self-esteem items:
- Do you feel you are as important as most people?
- Can you do things as well as others?

Social self-esteem items:
- Do you have only a few friends?
- Do most people respect your views?

Personal self-esteem items:
- Are your feelings easily hurt?
- Are you as nice looking as most people?

Stability. Once a level of self-esteem is established, it tends to be stable and fairly resistant to change. Consequently, we find high correlations between an individual's self-esteem when it is assessed from time to time over the years. For instance, Coopersmith (1967) found a correlation coefficient of .70 between the pre- and posttest scores of 52 public school students for a three-year period. More recently, Savin-Williams and Demo (1983) studied adolescents, and found correlation coefficients ranging from .59 to .66 for students in seventh through tenth grades. I, too, found a correlation coefficient of .74 for 33 sixth-grade students over a two-year period (1977). These high correlation coefficients provide strong support for the position that asserts that self-esteem is a stable disposition.

Although self-esteem is mostly stable, change can occur during any developmental period. In order for significant change to occur, however, some form of intervention is required.

Gradual development. Self-esteem develops gradually as the child matures and interacts with other people who are important to him or her. Development of self-esteem commences during the first year of life and becomes stable about age ten. Self-esteem becomes more stabilized and differentiated with age.

Parents exert the greatest influence on the development of a child's self-esteem; the child's self-esteem mirrors to a great extent the appraisals of parents or parent-surrogates. Teachers also have a strong effect, because once the child enters school, the teacher functions "in loco parentis," sharing many of the responsibilities of parents.

Personality: A Guiding Force

Personality is a phenomenon which is difficult to define, because experts tend to emphasize different properties in their definitions. For instance, some authorities emphasize social factors, or how the individual appears to others, as being the major determinants of personality; others emphasize characteristics or qualities within the individual. Some theorists stress uniqueness and distinguishing characteristics of the individual; others emphasize the organizing functions of the personality; and still others use concepts such as "essence" and "character" to describe personality.

Although disagreement exists among psychologists regarding what personality is, there is nevertheless some degree of consensus among them. Authorities generally support three groups of views regarding personality. One group views personality as being an organization of various systems within the individual that determine his characteristic behavior; another group emphasizes behavioral and environmental determinants of personality; yet another group of experts emphasizes subjective awareness as a major factor determining personality.

The most commonly quoted definition of personality is the one provided by Allport (1961), in which he defines personality as being:

> . . . The dynamic organization within the individual of those psychophysical systems that determine his characteristic behavior and thought.

I view personality as being a derivative of the self, which represents the self's unique mode of adjusting to environmental demands. I consider personality to be a stable aspect of the psyche that predisposes the individual toward behaving in certain distinctive ways.

Personality emerges as the developing child introjects (that is, incorporates into himself) beliefs regarding himself and the world from significant others (usually parents) as he matures and interacts with them. These introjected values affect the child's personality and, subsequently, his self-esteem; this, in turn, affects his behavior and views regarding himself and his world. Personality is the major component of the psyche determining self-esteem, which is a consequence of early interactions with significant others. Once the values of significant others, that affect personality, are adopted, the child has acquired "conditions of worth"— which implies that the child cannot regard himself or herself positively (i.e., as being a worthwhile individual) unless behavior is consistent with the terms of these introjected values.

Self-Esteem Characteristics: High and Low

Characteristics of high self-esteem. The most comprehensive list of characteristics associated with high self-esteem are those provided by Coopersmith (1967). In *Antecedents of Self-Esteem*, Coopersmith proposed the following characteristics he considered to be associated with individuals experiencing high self-esteem. Coopersmith felt that:

1. Individuals with high self-esteem tend to be more effective in meeting environmental demands than those with low self-esteem.
2. People with high self-esteem tend to adopt an active and assertive position in meeting environmental demands.
3. High self-esteem is associated with such terms as self-respect, superiority, pride, self-acceptance, and self-love.
4. People with high self-esteem tend to be more autonomous, and generally manifest greater confidence that they will succeed, than individuals who possess low self-esteem.
5. High self-esteem individuals tend to be popular with their peers.
6. An individual with high self-esteem is apt to attend to others only to the extent that he esteems them.
7. High self-esteem individuals tend to participate in more exploratory and independent activities than do individuals with low self-esteem.
8. High self-esteem individuals tend to defend themselves well against threats and demeaning attempts by others.
9. High self-esteem individuals tend to possess greater confidence in their ability to deal with events; anxiety is less likely to be aroused in them; and they tend to have a greater ability to resist the negative implications of social judgments.

High self-esteem: a schematic profile. The child with high self-esteem generally considers himself or herself to be capable of dealing effectively with the demands of the internal and external environments. Thus, this child perceives that he is loved by significant others (especially parents), and that he is worthy of this love. The child with high self-esteem considers interpersonal relationships with peers to be positive and mutually beneficial, and typically feels that peers regard him highly and respect his point of view. The child with high self-esteem typically feels that he is at least as smart as his chronological age-mates, and generally reports that he is satisfied with his performance at school. The evolution of high self-esteem is schematically presented in Figure 2:1. Figure 2:1 is a theoretical conceptual progression of the development of high self-esteem in children.

FIGURE 2:1. *Schematic Presentation of the Development of High Self-Esteem.*

Positive parental interactions
Unconditional positive regard
Accurate perceptions of self-worth
High self-esteem

Characteristics of low self-esteem. Coopersmith provided the following characteristics of individuals experiencing low self-esteem:

1. Individuals with low self-esteem tend to withdraw from others and experience consistent feelings of distress.
2. People with low self-esteem tend to be more intropunitive (i.e., "being hard on oneself") and passive in adapting to environmental demands and pressures than individuals who possess high self-esteem.
3. Low self-esteem tends to be equated with inferiority, timidity, self-hatred, lack of personal acceptance, and submissiveness.
4. People low in self-esteem tend to exhibit higher levels of anxiety and are more likely to exhibit more frequent psychosomatic symptoms and feelings of depression than individuals with high self-esteem.
5. People with low self-esteem tend to be isolates who seldom select one another. These individuals tend to feel that they have greater difficulties in forming friendships than do others. There does not appear

to be any relationship, however, between self-esteem and group membership. Persons of all levels of confidence and assurance are equally likely to join social groups; but the roles they play are different.

6. Low self-esteem individuals tend not to resist social pressures.

7. Individuals with low self-esteem are more likely to remain quiet if they feel dissent will evoke personal attack. They are often unwilling to express controversial opinions, even when they know they are correct; and they tend to have strong, defensive reactions to criticism.

8. Low self-esteem individuals tend to be "invisible" members of a group; they rarely serve as leaders.

9. Low self-esteem individuals tend to lack confidence to respect the critical appraisal of others, and remain defeated and exposed in their real or imagined deficiencies.

10. Individuals with low self-esteem tend to be self-conscious when talking to others. They tend to be quite conscious of their inadequacies—whether real or imagined.

11. Low self-esteem individuals, when distracted by personal concerns, will likely turn inward and dwell upon themselves—unlike those with high self-esteem.

In addition to Coopersmith's list, I believe that the following are additional characteristics of individuals who possess low self-esteem (1982, pp. 41-43):

1. Low self-esteem individuals tend to be low in initiative and basically nonassertive in their interactions with others.

2. Low self-esteem individuals tend to be more anxious than individuals who possess high self-esteem. These individuals tend to worry and to be pessimistic in their views concerning the future.

3. Low self-esteem individuals tend to be more prone to employing the defenses of projection and repression than individuals who esteem themselves highly.

4. Low self-esteem individuals tend to be more susceptible to developing obsessive-compulsive reactions than people who esteem themselves highly.
5. Low self-esteem individuals tend to be more timid, shy, and predisposed to withdrawal than individuals who esteem themselves highly.
6. Low self-esteem people tend to be indecisive and usually vacillate when confronted with obstacles.
7. Low self-esteem individuals are more prone to emitting self-defeating responses and developing self-punishing modes of behavior than individuals who esteem themselves highly.
8. Low self-esteem individuals tend to conform more readily to social pressure and exhibit a greater degree of dependence than individuals who esteem themselves highly.

Low self-esteem: a schematic profile. Children with low self-esteem generally possess pessimistic views regarding themselves and their ability to exert a significant effect on their environment. The youngster with low self-esteem typically does not consider himself to be as competent as his chronological age mates and generally lacks confidence in his ability to perform academic tasks. These children tend to display a dysphoric (unhappy) disposition, and they typically feel that parents and other significant others do not love and prize them as much as they should. The child with low self-esteem usually experiences difficulties in his or her interpersonal interactions with peers and rarely assumes positions of leadership.

Figure 2:2 presents a schematic theoretical conceptual progression of the development of low self-esteem in children.

FIGURE 2:2. *Schematic Presentation of the Development of Low Self-Esteem.*

Negative parental interactions
Conditional regard
Distorted perceptions of self-worth
Low self-esteem

Self-Appraisals

The self-appraisals of children and adults with average self-esteem tend to fall somewhere between the high and low extremes, with some responses reflecting high self-esteem and some reflecting the opposite. After the child progresses through adolescence and emerges as an adult, his or her high or low self-esteem may be reflected in the following fashion.

A person thinking well of oneself is likely to say something like this:

I consider myself a valuable and important person, and am at least as good as other people of my age and training. I am regarded as someone worthy of respect and consideration by people who are important to me. I'm able to exert an influence upon other people and events, partly because my views are sought and respected, and partly because I'm able and willing to present and defend those views. I have a pretty definite idea of what I think is right, and my judgments are usually borne out by subsequent events. I can control my actions toward the outside world, and have a fairly good understanding of the kind of person I am. I enjoy new and challenging tasks, and don't get upset when things don't go well right off the bat. The work I do is generally of high quality, and I expect to do worthwhile and possibly great work in the future.

A person with a low opinion of self is likely to say things like this:

I don't think I'm a very important or likeable person, and I don't see much reason for anyone else to like me. I can't do many things I'd like to do, or do them the way I think they should be done. I'm not sure of my ideas or abilities, and there's a good likelihood that other people's ideas and work are better than my own. Other people don't pay much attention to me; and, given what I know and feel about myself, I can't say that I blame them. I don't like new or unusual occurrences, and prefer sticking to known and safe ground. I don't expect much from myself, either now or in the future. Even when I try very hard, the results are often poor, and I've just about given up hope that I'll do anything important or worthwhile. I don't have much control over what happens to me and I expect that things will get worse rather than better.

Responses reflecting self-esteem: high and low. The child with high self-esteem typically answers "yes" to the following statements incorporated in the *Culture-Free Self-Esteem Inventory for Children*, whereas the child with low self-esteem generally answers "no":

- . I am happy most of the time.
- Boys and girls like to play with me.
- I can do things as well as other boys and girls.
- My parents understand how I feel.

The Parent's Role and Self-Esteem

Of all influences, parents have the strongest effect on the self-esteem of their children; and the interaction between parent and child (the parent-child interactive process) is the most important variable affecting children's self-esteem. How parents treat their children determines whether the children will develop high, low, or intermediate levels of self-esteem.

In general, if parents communicate to their children that they love them unconditionally and interact with them in a nonpunitive fashion, children will develop high levels of self-esteem. However, if parents communicate to their children that their love for them has conditions placed upon it, children will develop low levels of self-esteem.

The roles that parents assume in the family constellation tend to exert differential effects on the self-esteem of boys and girls. For instance, if Mom assumes a dominant role, and the father a passive one, these dispositions tend to have a positive effect on the girl's self-esteem, but a negative effect on the boy's self-esteem. Conversely, if Dad assumes a dominant role and Mom a passive one, this tends to have a positive effect on the boy's self-esteem, but a negative effect on the girl's. If both parents interact in a democratic fashion, and assume equal amounts of authority and responsibility, these dispositions generally have positive effects on the self-esteem of both boys and girls. The reverse, of course, is equally true: If both parents are punitive and interact with their children in an autocratic fashion, this will have negative effects on the self-esteem of both boys and girls.

SUMMARY

1. Although there is considerable controversy regarding what self-esteem is, most experts think that self esteem refers to an individual's perception of his or her own worth.
2. Self-esteem is a subjective, evaluative, multifaceted phenomenon that is stable and develops gradually.
3. Self-esteem is a stable phenomenon, but positive change can occur if effective intervention is provided.
4. Although experts disagree on the nature of one's personality, they generally agree that it is a powerful force affecting self-esteem.
5. The interaction between parent and child is the most important variable affecting children's self-esteem.
6. The roles that parents assume differentially affect the self-esteem of boys and girls.

II

SELF-ESTEEM AND ADJUSTMENT

Chapter 3

DISORDERED SELF-ESTEEM:
ETIOLOGY AND CONSEQUENCES

Etiology

Self-esteem is disordered when it is low resulting from extremely negative interactions between parent and child. In disordered self-esteem, the parent-interactive facet is always low, an observation that is necessary for diagnosis of this condition. In disordered self-esteem of adolescents, high school age and older, the personal facet of self-esteem is always low, and likewise a necessary condition for this diagnosis.

Although ineffective or negative interactions are associated with all forms of low self-esteem, children with disordered self-esteem are exposed to more pathological or intensely negative interactions with parents and people similarly important to them, than are others. The parent-child interactive process of the child with disordered self-esteem is characterized by rejection, conditional regard, and punitive reprimands. These young people feel unloved and powerless in their ability to obtain the care and respect they need and desire. This condition of disordered self-esteem often leads to emotional problems such as anxiety disorders and depression.

Although children who are generally low in self-esteem

experience symptoms similar to those of children with disordered self-esteem, the two groups (those with generally low self-esteem and those with disordered self-esteem) can be differentiated. First, the symptoms associated with disordered self-esteem are more intense and are generally due to more severely pathological interactions with parents. Second, the self-esteem profiles of the two groups tend to differ, because children with disordered self-esteem generally feel that their parents do not love and accept them as they are, whereas children with generally low self-esteem typically feel that their parents do love and accept them. Third, children with disordered self-esteem tend to be more gloomy and pessimistic regarding the present and future; the other group has a more hopeful and optimistic attitude.

Disordered Self-Esteem and Misbehavior

Children with disordered self-esteem are prime candidates for displaying misbehavior, and the goal of that is almost always revenge, because they desire to hurt parents who they perceive have hurt them. Children with disordered self-esteem, like other children in our society, however, find it difficult to attack their parents directly, because their psyches will not permit it. Because societal and parental conditioning does not permit the child to mount a frontal attack on parents, this child must attack them in subtle ways. Common methods used by children in their attempts to obtain revenge upon parents include behaviors such as sexual promiscuity and drug abuse. Although the child is not generally aware of the motives behind his or her behavior, the methods just mentioned generally inflict the greatest pain on parents.

Consequences of Disordered Self-Esteem

The consequences of disordered self-esteem in children and adolescents are varied, and include conditions such as underachievement (Wedemeyer 1953), learning problems (Battle 1975, 1979), and delinquency (Yeudall

1972). The most severe consequences of disordered self-esteem in children, however, are (1) childhood anxiety disorder, (2) childhood depression, and (3) childhood suicide.

Childhood anxiety disorder. Although there are numerous theoretical views that attempt to explain the causes of anxiety disorders, the most popular position is the one offered by Sigmund Freud, which assumes that anxiety is a symbolic manifestation of underlying unconscious psychological conflict. Despite the wide number of symptoms that are usually associated with anxiety disorders, there is no *single* cause. Simply, the individual with such unresolved conflict or conflicts is generally tense and apprehensive.

There are three groups of childhood anxiety disorders: (a) separation anxiety disorder, (b) shyness disorder, and (c) overanxious disorder.

Separation anxiety disorder. The youngster experiencing separation anxiety disorder refuses to leave individuals to whom he is emotionally attached (e.g., parents) because he fears that, if he does, something terrible will happen to them or to him. This condition is characterized by exaggerated distress at the separation from parents, home, or other familial surroundings.

The sleep pattern of children experiencing separation anxiety disorder is often disrupted by nightmares. They often report that they see and feel eyes staring at them in the dark; or that mythic-type, glaring, or bloody creatures are reaching for them (Battle 1983).

Shyness disorder. Children experiencing a shyness disorder try to avoid interactions with strangers and often display motor inhibition and lack of initiative. The major symptom, or characteristic of shyness disorder in children, is a persistent and excessive shrinking from familiarity or contact with strangers, which avoidance is severe enough to interfere with peer-functioning. Children experiencing shyness disorder are typically nonassertive, nonaggressive individuals who become tearful and anxious when pressured to interact with peers and participate in activities.

Overanxious disorder. Children experiencing an overanxious disorder generally question their ability to perform successfully; and they maintain a constant fear of failure. The main characteristic or symptom of this disorder is worrying and fearful behavior that is generally accompanied by physical signs: complaints of a lump in the throat, gastrointestinal distress, headaches, feelings of shortness of breath, cold, nauseousness, and dizziness. In addition, children with an overanxious disorder frequently experience sleep disturbances. For instance, they may experience difficulties in falling asleep or in too-early awakening with inability to get back to sleep.

Childhood depression. Depression is associated with low levels of self-esteem. Depression is a prominent, fairly persistent, and allied disorder–characterized by appetite disturbance, change in weight, sleep disturbance, psychomotor agitation or retardation or decreased energy, feelings of worthlessness or guilt, difficulty in concentrating or thinking, and thoughts of death or suicide or suicidal attempts (APA 1980, pp. 211-212).

Although controversy regarding the issue of depression in children continues, most experts assume that "depression as a clinical entity exists in children" (Kashani et al. 1981, p. 150). From this controversy among experts, the problem of depression in children has attracted the attention of researchers only recently. Only in the past few years has depression in children been studied extensively and systematically.

The reported incidence of depression in children ranges from as low as 1 percent to as high as 59 percent (Kashani et al. 1981). More recently, Paananen (1983) found the incidence of depression in children to range from 2 to 10 percent. Strong support for the position which proposes that school-age children experience depression is provided by Paananen in her 1983 study, in which she employed 620 students in grades four through six. Paananen identified two groups of subjects in her study (depressed and nondepressed), and administered the *Culture-Free Self-Esteem Inventory for Children*, Form A (Battle 1981), and two measures of depression to all participants. As predicted, Paananen found that depressed children earned lower self-esteem scores on all facets of self-esteem than their nondepressed counterparts, with the highest correlations being between parent-related self-esteem and depression. Findings of Paananen's study are summarized in Table 3:1.

TABLE 3:1. *Means, Standard Deviations, and Significance for Depressed and Nondepressed Subjects.*

| | Depressed Group | | Nondepressed Group | | |
	Mean	S.D.	Mean	S.D.	p
Total	25.55	7.60	46.61	2.69	.001
General	9.91	3.36	19.11	1.17	.001
Social	4.27	2.36	8.46	1.24	.001
Acad.	5.80	2.61	9.42	.95	.001
Parental	5.57	2.74	9.62	.80	.001
Total	23.20	7.97	47.12	2.65	.001
General	8.40	3.25	19.12	1.42	.001
Social	3.96	2.19	8.36	1.38	.001
Acad.	5.52	2.55	9.68	.63	.001
Parental	5.32	2.87	9.96	.20	.001

Source: Paananen, N. R. 1983. Incidence and characteristics of depression in late childhood: an exploratory study. Doctoral dissertation. Edmonton, Alberta: University of Alberta. Reproduced by permission.

In 1983, I studied the relationship between self-esteem and depression in children in grades four through nine who were referred to me for assessment. Sixty percent of the children were referred because teachers felt they were experiencing emotional problems (e.g., anxiety disorders or depression); 40 percent were referred for behavior problems (e.g., deviant behavior, impulsiveness). I individually administered the *Culture-Free Self-Esteem Inventory for Children* and a modified version of Beck's *Depression Scale* to all participating subjects, and found self-esteem to be significantly related to depression in children. Findings of the study are summarized in Table 3:2.

The data presented in Table 3:2 clearly indicate that depression is significantly related to all facets of self-esteem. The parent-interaction facet of self-esteem, however, relates more highly with depression than other facets (e.g., social, academic) for all groups, indicating that the relationship be-

TABLE 3.2. *Correlations and Significance, 1983 Study.*

	Total r	Elem. r	Jr. High r	p
Total	−.83	−.86	−.83	.01
General	−.75	−.79	−.75	.01
Social	−.44	−.65	−.35	.01
Academic	−.62	−.60	−.62	.01
Parental	−.66	−.75	−.64	.01

tween parent and child is the most important one affecting the mental health of young people.

I also studied the relationship between self-esteem and depression in college students (1978). In that study, I administered the *Culture-Free Self-Esteem Inventory for Adults* and Beck's instrument to all participants, and found that self-esteem was significantly related to depression for the total sample, males and females. Findings are presented in Table 3:3.

As one might expect, the data in Table 3:3 indicate that self-esteem is significantly related to depression in this way: As self-esteem increases, depression decreases.

In another study, I studied the relationship between self-esteem and depression in high school students (1980). In the study, I administered the *Culture-Free Self-Esteem Inventory for Adults*, Beck's inventory, and the Depression subscale of a short form of the *Minnesota Multiphasic Personality Inventory* (MMPI) to all subjects, and found that all facets of self-esteem were significantly related to depression as measured by both Beck's scale and the MMPI. Findings of the study appear in Table 3:4.

The data presented in Table 3:4 confirm previous findings which indicate that there is a significant relationship between self-esteem and depression, with the personal or parental-related facet being most highly related.

The case studies reported in the next few pages, following, illustrate the relationship between disordered self-esteem and depression in children, adolescents, and adults of various ages.

TABLE 3:3. Means, Standard Deviations, and Correlations of Two Measures by Sex (N = 129; n = 43 males, n = 86 females).

	Combined Sexes				Males				Females			
	Mean	S.D.	r	p	Mean	S.D.	r	p	Mean	S.D.	r	p
Self-Esteem	24.17	5.10	−.55	.01	24.53	4.69	−.53	.01	23.98	5.31	−.56	.01
Depression	4.57	3.84			4.41	3.48			4.65	4.03		

Note: High self-esteem scores indicate positive self-esteem; low depression scores indicate lack of depression.

TABLE 3:4. Means, Standard Deviations, and Correlations for All Subjects (N = 26).

	Self-Esteem		Depression				MMPI			
	Mean	S.D.	Mean	S.D.	r	p	Mean	S.D.	r	p
Total	16.69	7.46	15.13	12.12	−.75	.01	28.00	6.19	−.75	.01
General	8.03	4.21	15.13	12.12	−.78	.01	28.00	6.19	−.72	.01
Social	5.15	1.82	15.13	12.12	−.34	.05	28.00	6.19	−.42	.01
Personal	3.46.	2.73	15.13	12.12	−.61	.01	28.00	6.19	−.73	.01

Note: High self-esteem scores indicate positive self-esteem; low depression scores indicate lack of depression.

Case Report 3:1. Harold D.; 9 years, 9 months. Disordered self-esteem and depression.

Harold was the oldest of two children in a family. His mother reported that the delivery was difficult but that the birth process was normal. Development during the first five years was generally normal. Harold walked at 9 months, started to use sentences at 16 months, and was toilet trained at 3 years.

Harold was enrolled in kindergarten at the age of four and a half. Adjustment in kindergarten and up through grade three was generally satisfactory; but his teachers felt he could earn better grades. Harold, however, experienced considerable academic difficulties in fourth grade. At this point Harold was referred to a psychologist who diagnosed him as being a depressed child who possessed low self-esteem. His scores on the *Wechsler Intelligence Scale for Children, Revised* (WISC-R) Verbal, Performance, and Full Scale IQ scores were 130, 118, and 127 respectively. Analysis of self-esteem scores revealed the following:

Score

	Possible	Mean	Actual	%-ile	t	Class.
Total	50	35.7	14	1	33	v. low
General	20	14.2	7	6	33	low
Social	10	7.1	5	32	46	inter.
Academic	10	7.0	1	21	27	v. low
Parental	10	7.4	1	1	22	v. low

Case Report 3:2. Bambi J.: 14 years, 10 months. Disordered self-esteem and depression.

Bambi was the only child of middle-age parents. Her mother reported that the pregnancy and birth process were normal. With the exception of being overly active, Bambi's development during the first four years of her life was generally normal. Bambi walked at 11 months, started to use words at 18 months, and was toilet trained at 2 years, 8 months. When she was three, Bambi's parents separated. Shortly afterwards, she was diagnosed by her pediatrician as being "hyperactive." The drug Ritalin was prescribed; but Bambi's mother refused to administer the medication to her. Bambi made passing grades during the elementary and junior high school years, but her teachers commented that she could have earned better grades if she had been able to sustain her attention more effectively.

At the age of 14, Bambi attempted suicide by taking an overdose of sleeping pills. She was treated in a hospital overnight and released the next day. Upon her release, her mother referred her to a psychologist for psychotherapy. Bambi's WISC-R Verbal, Performance, and Full Scale IQ scores were 100, 111, and 105 respectively. Personality test results indicated that this client was depressed and possessed very low self-esteem. Analysis of the self-esteem scores revealed the following:

		Score				
	Possible	Mean	Actual	%-ile	*t*	Class.
Total	32	23.7	13	6	33	v. low
General	16	12.0	5	5	32	v. low
Social	8	6.9	7	78	59	high
Personal	8	4.9	1	14	38	v. low

Case Report 3:3. Henry M.; 16 years, 5 months.
Disordered self-esteem and depression.

Henry was a 16-year-old tenth-grade student who was the only adopted child in a family with six children. Henry first experienced learning problems in the form of reading and arithmetic disabilities when he was in second grade. At this time he was assessed by educational specialists and was subsequently placed in the resource room program. He nevertheless continued to make only marginal academic progress.

Henry presented fairly severe behavioral problems in school during the fourth grade. He was referred for psychiatric treatment at this time and was placed on Ritalin. Chemotherapy, however, was not effective.

Henry repeated the fourth grade, and ninth grade as well. He was referred to the reporting psychologist during his second year of ninth grade. In the initial interview process, he appeared to be a child of average intelligence who was experiencing considerable adjustment difficulties. He was depressed, alienated, and was entertaining thoughts of suicide. He was irritated with himself. An analysis of his self-esteem revealed the following:

. . . .

		Score				
	Possible	Mean	Actual	%-ile	t	Class.
Total	32	23.7	6	1	17	v. low
General	16	12.0	2	1	16	v. low
Social	8	6.9	4	11	37	inter.
Personal	8	4.9	0	14	37	v. low

. . . .

Case Report 3:4. Bobby B; 28 years, married.
Disordered self-esteem and depression.

Bobby was the only boy in a family with four children. Bobby made passing marks during the elementary, junior high, and high school years; but his teachers generally commented that they felt he could make better grades. His interactions with peers were fairly typical during the formative years; but Bobby lacked initiative and perseverence; and he rarely assumed leadership roles. After three years of study, at three different universities, he had accumulated only a few credits. After his dismissal from the third university, Bobby contacted a psychologist and requested therapy because "he couldn't understand why he continually failed." His *Wechsler Adult Intelligence Scale* (WAIS) Verbal, Performance, and Full Scale IQ scores were 123, 122, and 124 respectively. Personality test results indicated that the client was depressed and possessed very low self-esteem. Analysis of self-esteem scores revealed the following:

. . . .

Score

	Possible	Mean	Actual	%-ile	t	Class.
Total	32	23.7	11	2	27	v. low
General	16	12.0	5	2	27	low
Social	8	6.9	5	30	44	inter.
Personal	8	4.9	1	14	37	v. low

. . . .

Childhood suicide. Negative interactions and the stress associated with our rapidly changing society heavily tax the coping strategies of developing children and youth, and make it difficult for them to develop appropriately and maintain a high degree of self-esteem. For instance, depression among children and adolescents, which is generally associated with low self-esteem (Battle 1978, 1980), has increased significantly during the last decade. Suicide, which typically follows depression, is among the leading causes of death of North American youth. Although auto accidents are the number-one cause of death, many experts feel that many of the fatalities are in reality self-induced. Thus, a greater number of youth deaths can be attributed to suicide than statistics generally indicate.

Although the actual number of children who commit suicide is low, 7 to 10 percent of children referred to child psychiatric clinics have threatened or attempted suicide (Shaffer 1974).

Although experts are becoming more knowledgeable

regarding the problems of suicide, there continue to exist many myths. Some of the most popular myths about suicide are presented in Figure 3:1, with corresponding facts to counteract each myth.

FIGURE 3:1. *Suicide: Facts and Fables.*

Fable: People who talk about suicide don't commit suicide.

Fact: Of any ten people who kill themselves, eight have given definite warnings of their suicidal intentions.

Fable: Suicide happens without warning.

Fact: Studies reveal that the suicidal person gives many clues and warnings regarding his suicidal intentions.

Fable: Suicidal people are fully intent on dying.

Fact: Most suicidal people are undecided about living or dying; and they "gamble with death," leaving it to others to save them. Almost no one commits suicide without letting others know how he is feeling.

Fable: Once a person is suicidal, he is suicidal forever.

Fact: Individuals who wish to kill themselves are "suicidal" for only a short period of time.

Fable: Improvement following a suicidal crisis means that the suicidal risk is over.

Fact: Most suicides occur within about three months following the beginning of "improvement," when the individual has the energy to put his morbid thoughts and feelings into effect.

Fable: Suicide strikes much more often among the rich— or, conversely, it occurs almost exclusively among the poor.

Fact: Suicide is neither the rich man's disease nor the poor man's curse. Suicide is very "democratic" and is represented proportionately among all levels of society.

Fable: Suicide is inherited or "runs in the family."

Fact: Suicide does not run in families. It is an individual pattern.

Fable: All suicidal individuals are mentally ill, and suicide is always the act of a psychotic person.

Fact: Studies of hundreds of genuine suicide notes indicate that, although the suicidal person is extremely unhappy, he is not necessarily mentally ill.

Source: Shneidman, E. S., and Farberow, N. L. 1961. Government Printing Office: PHS Publication No. 852.

Although Shneidman and Farberow (1961) propose that suicide does not run in families, some characteristics do exist in families in which members commit suicide. Some common characteristics are:

1. Intolerance for separation: Many suicidal families experience more incidents of loss or separation than the general population; therefore, they are highly sensitive to any sort of separation; and the threat of separation may cause a family member to have a suicidal crisis.

2. Symbiosis without empathy: Symbiotic relationships are present, but exploitation is also involved. The family members do not see the needs of the suicidal person as separate from their own, and therefore do not recognize that person's individualism. When his needs are not met, the suicidal individual believes that he is "not to be."

3. Fixation upon infantile patterns: Suicidal families are threatened by the possible separation equated with growth, maturity, and change. They therefore attempt to stifle such growth by focusing on early, infantile patterns.

4. Fixation upon earlier social roles: Suicidal family members, especially parents, are often replaying social roles of an earlier time. As change in their present family occurs, conflict between new and old roles may cause a suicidal crisis.

5. Closed family system: A suicidal family does not encourage contact outside its nucleus, as this might threaten the status quo.

6. Aggression and death wishes directed against the potentially suicidal person by the family: This is a pattern which is expressed both verbally and nonverbally to the suicidal individual.

7. Scapegoating: This involves punitive isolation and alienation of the suicidal person.

8. Sadomasochistic relationships: Members of suicidal

families alternate between being hurt and hurting others.

9. Double-bind relationships: Anyone coming close is hurt, yet distance is not tolerated.
10. Family fragility: A suicidal family does not see itself as capable of coping with everyday living.
11. Suicidal person is the "bad object" for the family: In suicidal families, the suicidal individual is regarded as the activator of the forbidden desires and bad impulses of other family members.
12. Family depression: Suicidal families are often preoccupied with death and therefore exhibit depressive symptoms.
13. Communication disturbances: There is no awareness of the messages and feelings of other family members, especially the suicidal individual.
14. Intolerance for crisis: Suicidal families cannot tolerate any crisis which affects their everyday lifestyle.

Most children who commit suicide will have discussed, threatened, or attempted suicide previously. The majority of youths who commit suicide are socially isolated and come from homes in which parents are divorced. The majority of young people who commit suicide experience alienation and lack of authentic caring relationships with significant others. These youngsters typically experience academic difficulties in school. For instance, Rohn and fellow researchers (1977) studied adolescents who had attempted suicide and found that one of every five subjects had failed at least one grade, one third were dropouts or chronic truants, and another third experienced behavior problems at school. Precipitating factors compiled by Shaffer (1974, p 279) in the suicides of 31 children under the age of 15 are presented in Table 3:5.

The description of the suicidal youngsters listed here provides common characteristics of one group of young people; however, there is another group which possesses altogether different characteristics. In this group, the suicidal youngster tends to be above average in intelligence; quiet and difficult to know; perfectionistic and self-critical. This group, however, does share the one characteristic of social isolation with the earlier group (Shaffer 1974). This type of

TABLE 3:5. *Precipitating Factors in the Suicide of Children.*

Type of Crisis	Boy	Girl	Total	%
Disciplinary crisis	8	3	11	36
Fight with peers other than close friend of opposite sex	3	1	4	13
Dispute with close friend of opposite sex	1	2	3	10
Dispute with parent	1	2	3	10
Being dropped from a school team	2	0	2	7
Fantasy "model"	1	1	2	7
Interaction with psychotic parent	2	0	2	7
No precipitation disclosed	3	0	3	10

Source: Shaffer, D. 1974. Suicide in childhood and early adolescence. *Journal of Child Psychology and Psychiatry* 15:275-291.

suicidal youngster is illustrated in the following news report.

A pre-med student with straight A's shot and killed his 10-year-old brother and then killed himself when his medical school application was rejected. A note he left said that he wanted to save his brother from having to live through the miserable years ahead of him.

Youth suicide victims often are depressed and generally are gloomy and pessimistic about the present and future, as illustrated in the following case of a teenage girl called Beverly:

Case Report 3:5. Beverly.
Youth suicide attempt.

Beverly decided to kill herself on St. Patrick's Day. She considered methods carefully. She had read about a window-washer who fell to his death a short time before. Since she had neither a gun nor drugs at her disposal, she decided to jump from her eighth-floor apartment window. She survived the fall and later told about her feelings. She had left her home on the east coast of the U.S. and had come to Seattle, as far away from home as she could get. She got a job in a cafeteria and stayed in her apartment the rest of the time.

"I hated myself. I felt stupid. I didn't like the way I looked. I wanted to be prettier, to be taller, to have a nicer nose and thicker hair. I stayed in my apartment most of the time. I was convinced that I didn't have anything to offer anybody else. I'd only end up getting hurt and rejected. I spent a lot of time thinking about what I wanted to do with myself. I saw my choices as going back to high school at night while working, going back to my family, or committing suicide. I thought all the choices were bad, but I thought suicide was the best."

The following poem was submitted to his twelfth-grade English teacher by a student who committed suicide two weeks later:

About School

He always wanted to say things. But no one understood.
He always wanted to explain things. But no one cared.
So he drew.

Sometimes he would just draw and it wasn't anything.
He wanted to carve it in stone or write it in the sky.
He would lie out on the grass and look up in the sky and it would be only him and the sky and the things inside that needed saying.

And it was after that, that he drew the picture. It was a beautiful picture. He kept it under the pillow and would let no one see it.
And he would look at it every night and think about it. And when it was dark, and his eyes were closed, he could still see it.
And it was all of him. And he loved it.

When he started school he brought it with him. Not to show to anyone, but just to have it with him like a friend.

It was funny about school.

He sat in a square, brown desk like all the other square, brown desks and he thought it should be red.

And his room was a square, brown room. Like all the other rooms. And it was tight and close. And stiff.

He hated to hold the pencil and the chalk, with his arm stiff and his feet flat on the floor, stiff, with the teacher watching and watching.

And then he had to write numbers. And they weren't anything. They were worse than the letters that could be something if you put them together.

And the numbers were tight and square and he hated the whole thing.

The teacher came and spoke to him. She told him to wear a tie like all the other boys. He said he didn't like them and she said it didn't matter.

After that they drew. And he drew all yellow and it was the way he felt about morning. And it was beautiful.

The teacher came and smiled at him. "What's this?" she said. "Why don't you draw something like Ken's drawing?

Isn't that beautiful?"

It was all questions.

After that his mother bought him a tie and he always drew airplanes and rocket ships like everyone else.

And he threw the old picture away.

And when he lay out alone looking at the sky, it was big and blue and all of everything, but he wasn't anymore.

He was all square inside and brown, and his hands were stiff, and he was like anyone else. And the thing inside him that needed saying didn't need saying anymore.

It had stopped pushing. It was crushed. Stiff.
Like everything else.

(Canfield and Wells 1976, p. 114)

Another group of young people, college students, tend to be quite susceptible to committing suicide. Depression, which often leads to suicide, is quite high among college students, affecting as many as 77 percent of pupils (Beck and Young 1978). The suicide rate for college students is at least 50 percent greater than it is for their non-college counterparts. More than 100,000 college students in the United States attempt suicide each year; and, of these, 1,000 actually kill themselves. In a widely publicized research project, Seiden (1966) studied college students at the University of California at Berkeley, and found that the students who committed suicide generally earned grades above the median grade-point average, but typically felt that they were not earning high enough grades. These students tended to perceive themselves negatively, developed depression, and subsequently committed suicide. The following case report of a 19-year-old college student illustrates typical sentiments such as feelings of rejection and a desire for revenge that are often experienced by suicidal youths.

Case Report 3:6. A letter from a suicidal student.

Dear Jim:

I've emptied 40 capsules and put the powder in a glass of water. I'm about to take it. I'm scared and I want to talk to someone, but I just don't have anybody to talk to. I know our break-up was my fault, but it hurts so bad. Nothing I do seems to turn out right, but nothing. My whole life has fallen apart, maybe if . . . but I know.

I've thought about all the trite phrases about how it will get brighter tomorrow and how suicide is copping out and really isn't a solution and maybe it isn't but I hurt so bad. I just want it to stop. I feel like my back is up against the wall and there is no other way out.

It's getting harder to think and my life is about to end. Tears are rolling down my face and I feel so scared and alone. Oh Jim . . . if you could put your arms around me and hold me close . . . just one last t...im....

A change in a student's mood and behavior is a significant warning of possible suicide. Characteristically, the student becomes depressed and withdrawn, undergoes a marked decline in self-esteem, and shows deterioration in habits of personal hygiene. This is accompanied by a profound loss of interest in studies. Often, he or she stops attending classes and stays at home most of the day. Usually, the student's distress is communicated to at least one other person, often in the form of a veiled suicide warning. A significant number of students who attempt suicide leave suicide notes.

When college students attempt suicide, one of the first explanations to occur to those around them is that they may have been doing poorly in school. As a group, however, they are superior students; and, while they tend to expect a great deal of themselves in terms of academic achievement and to exhibit scholastic anxieties, such things as grades, academic competition, and pressure over examinations are not regarded as significant precipitating stresses. Also, while many lose interest in their studies prior to the onset of suicidal behavior and their grades get lower, the loss of interest appears to be associated with depression and withdrawal caused by other problems. When academic failure does appear to trigger suicidal behavior, moreover—in a minority of cases—the actual cause of the behavior is generally considered to be loss of self-esteem and failure to live up to parental expectations, rather than the academic failure itself.

For most suicidal students, both male and female, the major precipitating stressor appears to be either the failure to establish, or the loss of, a close interpersonal relationship. Often the break-up of a romance is the key factor. It has also been noted that there are significantly more suicide attempts and successful suicides by students from families where there has been separation, divorce, or the death of a parent. A particularly important precipitating factor among college males appears to be the existence of a close emotional involvement with a parent that is threatened when the student becomes involved with another person in college and tries to break this "parental knot."

Although most colleges and universities have mental health facilities to assist distressed students, few suicidal students seek professional help. It is thus of vital importance for those around a suicidal student to notice the warning signs and try to obtain help (Hardin 1975; Miller 1975; Murray 1973; Nelson 1971; Pausnau and Russell 1975; Peck and Schrut 1971; Shneidman, Parker, and Funkhouser 1970; Stanley and Barter 1970).

Parents and loved ones should note any significant deviation from the normal pattern of behavior, because deviation may indicate a tendency toward suicide. Additional warning signs include:

1. A sudden mood swing from depression to elation does not necessarily indicate improvement in a suicidal patient. The new happiness may mean that the person has finally reached a decision about his or her fate, and feels that a good decision has been found. Furthermore, once a person has moved out of a depressed state, that individual may have more energy to actually attempt the act of suicide (Mehr 1983).
2. Most people who kill themselves do talk about it or give some sort of warning sign. Even if death is joked about, the recurring mention of it should be investigated.
3. A lack of interest in activities that used to engage the individual indicates depression and should be noted (Battle 1985).
4. The use of drugs and alcohol may indicate the presence of unsolvable problems and the need to escape.
5. A change in eating patterns, whether it invloves loss of appetite or increased eating, may be a danger sign (Hart and Keidel 1979).
6. Sleep disturbance is also a possible symptom of suicidal ideation (Hart and Keidel 1979).
7. An unusually long grief reaction or depressive feelings over an extended period of time indicates deep-rooted problems (Hart and Keidel 1979).
8. Academic decline should be noted (Hart and Keidel 1979).

SUMMARY

1. Disordered self-esteem is a consequence of extremely negative interactions between parent and child.
2. Children with disordered self-esteem invariably display misbehavior.
3. Important consequences of disordered self-esteem are childhood anxiety disorder, childhood depres-

sion, and childhood suicide.
4. Suicide is the number-three killer of North American youth of 15 to 24 years of age.

Chapter 4

REMEDIATING DISORDERED SELF-ESTEEM

In the preceding chapter we described disordered self-esteem and listed some of its consequences. In this chapter, we will discuss means of remediating disordered self-esteem. At this point in our history it is commonplace to discuss remediation of learning disabilities in children and youth; but educators and other caretakers rarely propose remediation of self-esteem—the most important variable affecting the lives of children and adults at all stages of development. Youngsters experiencing disordered self-esteem require its remediation in the same fashion that children with learning disabilities require remediation of those disabilities.

I have stated elsewhere (1981, 1982) that it is essential for parents and educators to attend to the self-esteem needs of children in order to assist them in developing their potential fully. Educators, however, have all too frequently tended to ignore the self-esteem needs of children, while concentrating on their cognitive needs. This lack or awareness, or concern, has resulted in the escalation of many problems among school-age children—including underachievement, absenteeism, alienation, and juvenile delinquency.

The original source of responsibility for the development of disordered self-esteem, is the home, in which negative interactions take place between parent and child. The objective in the remediation of disordered self-esteem is to improve the child's self-esteem to the extent that it will enable him or her to develop effectively. The three important sources of remediation that may be required in order to assist a child in resolving his or her condition of disordered self-esteem are parents, teachers, and psychotherapists.

Parents

The child's perception of himself is greatly influenced by his relations with his parents or parent surrogates. In our North American culture, mothers or mother surrogates play the most significant role in the life of young children. Mothers are therefore generally the most important determinants of the self-esteem of their children. The mother is a major force which determines if her child will view him- or herself positively or negatively. A well-known theorist, Sullivan (1949), provided support for this position when he stated that "the self-system has its origins in interpersonal relationships and is influenced profoundly by reflected appraisals." Sullivan considered that, if parents communicate to their child the feeling that he is approved of, respected, and liked, he will develop a sense of self-acceptance and respect for himself and others as well. Conversely, if parents communicate to the child that he is not worthy, and generally tend to belittle him, blame him, and reject him, he will tend to view himself as being unworthy.

Rogers (1951), even earlier, provided support for the notion that parents are most important in the development of self-esteem in their children, when he stated that parents should provide their children with *unconditional* positive regard rather than *conditional* positive regard. Rogers urges parents to let their child know that he is loved, accepted, wanted, simply because "he is who he is," and that this prizing, loving, caring-for, is not conditional or dependent on the behavior the child emits (Battle 1982, pp. 31-32).

In their attempts to promote the development of high

self-esteem in their children, parents should provide for them: (1) positive parent-child relationships, (2) enforced limits, and (3) a democratic home environment. *Positive parent-child relationships.* Such a relationship is one characterized by mutual respect and positive interactions. Parents who interact positively and effectively with their children provide them unconditional positive regard and to communicate to them that they are unique individuals who possess the same basic rights as other humans. *Enforced limits.* Effective parents provide their children clearly defined limits that are enforced consistently. They provide a home structure which is needed in order to promote the development of competence—a necessary ingredient of self-esteem. *Democratic home environment.* Parents should establish a home environment for their children which provides respect and an opportunity for individual actions within the clearly defined limits just described. Parents who provide a democratic home environment for their children permit them to communicate their views openly without fear of rejection and reprimand.

In their interactions with their children, parent should provide them with (a) unconditional positive regard, (b) encouragement, and (c) reflective listening. *Unconditional positive regard.* Unconditional positive regard, as put forth by Rogers (1951), is a process in which parents communicate to their children that they are loved unconditionally. That is, they communicate to their children that caring for and prizing them is not contingent on any predetermined conditions. Children who have this from their parents realize that their parents love them at all times, even when they behave in a fashion that their parents consider to be inappropriate.

A question that parents frequently ask is, "How can I know if my children feel they are loved unconditionally?" We can never know with absolute certainty how another person perceives the world. If we listen to and observe our children's behavior closely, however, we can make reliable inferences regarding how they view themselves and others. Two examples are provided as illustrations of how we can determine if our children perceive that they are loved unconditionally.

Because my wife Dorothy and I feel that communication of unconditional positive regard is so critical, we made concerted efforts to make it as clear as possible to our children at a very early stage in their development that our love for them was without conditions, provided freely, simply because they were our children. For instance, when our daughter Christina was between the ages of two and a half and five, whenever I disciplined her (e.g., I rapped her on her hands approximately four times during this period), I would tell her that I loved her but that I was "spanking" her because I felt her behavior required that form of intervention. When our son, Jamie, was the same age, I rapped his hands perhaps eight to ten times; and when I applied this form of discipline to Jamie, Christina would put her arms around him and say, "Now, Jamie, he loves you; he just didn't like what you did." The observation led me to conclude that Christina knows she is loved unconditionally. When I tuck Jamie into bed at night, I kiss him and say, "Good night, Son; your Dad loves you." His reply is always, "I know; I love you, too, Dad." That leads me to conclude that Jamie knows he is loved unconditionally.

Encouragement. I recommend that parents consistently encourage their children as they interact with them. Parents who encourage their children emphasize positives rather than negatives. They minimize the importance of children's mistakes while recognizing and helping to build their assets and strengths.

Although there are many techniques that parents can use to encourage their children, Dinkmeyer and McKay (1976), in their parents' handbook, proposed that the most effective method to encourage youngsters is to employ certain types of phrases, such as those that:

1. Demonstrate acceptance—"I'm glad you enjoy learning"; "I like the way you did that."
2. Show confidence—"I have confidence in your judgment."
3. Focus on contributions, assets, and appreciation— "Thanks, I really appreciate you doing that because it makes my job much easier."
4. Recognize effort and improvement—"You're improving in . . . ."

The technique of reflective listening is yet another important technique that parents can use in their attempts to promote the development of positive perceptions of self-worth in their children.

Reflective listening. Reflective listening is the technique in which parents communicate to their child that they recognize the feelings behind "what he is saying" and "what he is not saying."

Reflective listening is a process which involves grasping what the child feels and means, and then stating or reflecting this meaning in a fashion so that the child feels understood and accepted. Thus, the technique of reflective listening works as a sort of mirror that enables the child to see him- or herself more clearly. It provides feedback. For example, the child may say, "The teacher is unfair. I'll never do well in her class." To reflect the child's feelings, the parent may say, "You're feeling angry and disappointed about school."

Parents—and, in fact, all advocates of children—can use the technique of reflective listening to assist children in obtaining resolutions to problems. As I have said elsewhere (1985), there are three basic steps involved in effective problem resolution:

1. Reflect the child's feelings so that he or she feels accepted and understood.
2. Help the child clarify the confronting problem with precision.
3. Help the child resolve the problem by:
   a. Exploring alternatives.
   b. Assessing the consequences of alternatives.
   c. Choosing modes of behavior that are self-enhancing rather than self-defeating.

Let's use "Jennifer" to illustrate how the three basic steps involved in the reflective listening process can be used to help children solve problems.

Jennifer, a 12-year-old, eighth-grade student, very emotionally says to her mother, "I hate Mr. Brown! He's a mean teacher!"

Step 1 (reflection): To reflect Jennifer's feelings, her mother may say, "It appears that things are not going well in Mr. Brown's class."

Step 2 (clarification): Jennifer may say, "Well, it's really not Mr. Brown who is the problem. It's Mary and Becky who bug me in Mr. Brown's class."

Step 3 (resolution): Jennifer's mother may say, "What do you think you can do to stop Mary and Becky from bugging you in Mr. Brown's class?"

Jennifer can then (a) explore some alternatives:

- "I can skip Mr. Brown's class."
- "I can ask Mr. Brown to assign me a desk that is not near Mary and Becky."

At that point, Jennifer's mother may say, "What do you feel would happen if you skipped Mr. Brown's class?" By asking this, she is (b) exploring consequences.

Jennifer may say, "I would probably fail the course."

Going on, Jennifer's mother may say, "What do you think would happen if you asked Mr. Brown to move your desk?"

Jennifer may say, "He would probably move it. Then Mary and Becky would not be able to bug me."

To help Jennifer (c) choose modes of behavior that are self-enhancing rather than self-defeating, Jennifer's mother might then say, "What do you feel is best? What choice will work best for you?"

Jennifer would probably say, "To ask Mr. Brown to assign me a desk that is not near Mary and Becky."

Teachers

Teachers play a major role in the promotion of self-esteem once children enter school, because teachers function "in loco parentis," sharing many of the responsibilities of parents (Battle 1981, 1983). Although parents exert the greatest effect on their children, once the child enters school, teachers become the most significant people affecting the self-esteem of their pupils. Of this, Labenne and Green said (1969, p. 27):

> Any person who is intimately involved in the administration of rewards and punishments is in a position to become a significant other . . . . It is not merely the ability or responsibility of administering the system . . .

that makes a teacher a significant other. Rather, it is the manner in which she uses her authority that causes her to have a potent impact.

Although empirical data are generally lacking regarding the effectiveness of many strategies which teachers assume are effective methods of enhancing the self-esteem of pupils, I feel that any procedure resulting in the development of a more positive teacher-pupil interactive process has the potential to enhance the self-esteem of participating pupils. The teacher-pupil interactive process is one in which the teacher lets the pupil know that:

He is an individual who is worthy and significant . . . and that this evaluation is not contingent on any predetermined conditions. It is a process in which the teacher provides structure for the child . . . and communicates to him that he is expected to perform and behave in a certain fashion. It is also communicated to the child that he can determine whether or not he will function in the expected fashion . . . and that he will have to assume the responsibility for his actions (Battle 1982, pp. 23-24).

Teachers can establish this supportive, well-structured environment. Although teachers will obviously use different approaches in their attempts to establish positive teacher-pupil interactions, the strategies delineated in the following pages are intended to serve as models which may be used by elementary, junior high, and high school teachers. These examples focus on the the teacher's introduction on the first day of a new class, since "first impressions" set the tone for how the entire school term will progress.

Elementary level strategies. On the first day of class, the elementary school teacher might say something like this:

Welcome, boys and girls, to grade . . . . I am your teacher, Mrs. Jones. I would like each of you to know that I am very pleased and excited to have this opportunity to work with you this year. However, before we begin our work, I would like to have a brief discussion with you. I would like to start our discussion by sharing with you some of my feelings. First, I would like you to know that I care for and respect each one of you. Also, my caring for and respecting you is not due to any special reasons. I feel that each of you is important, and that teachers and students do the best schoolwork when they care for and respect each other. So, remember that I will always care for and respect you, even when there are problems. For instance, sometimes during the year, I will insist that some of you do certain things—maybe even things that you may not want to do. I will make you do these things because I feel they are best for you. I will, however, care for and respect you at all times—when things are going good and even when things are not going good. Second, I have expectations for each of you. For instance, I expect each of you to do your schoolwork and behave appropriately. Third, I would like to meet each of you. So, when I call your name, please raise your hand.

After the teacher calls the roll and recognizes each student, she might say, "Are there any questions or comments?" After the teacher entertains all questions and comments, regularly scheduled tasks may commence.

Junior high level strategies. On the first day of class, the junior high school teacher might say:

Welcome to grade . . . . I am Mr. Wilson, the homeroom teacher for section . . . . During this first class, I would like to do two things. First, I would like to meet each of you; and second, I would like to conduct a brief class discussion. [The teacher calls the roll, acknowledging each student individually.]

I would like to start our discussion by sharing with you some of my feelings. The first—and probably the most important—thing I would like to say is that I care for you and respect each of you individually. Also, I would like for each of you to know that my caring for and respecting you is not due to, or dependent on, any special conditions. I care for and respect you because you are who you are: simply because you are my pupils.

I would also like to say that I have expectations for you. For instance, I expect each of you to do your best school work, attend classes regularly, and behave appropriately. I realize that each of you will have to decide whether or not you will behave in the expected fashion; however, the decision about that is one that you must make. Only you can make this decision; and, of course, each of you will have to take responsibility for your decisions and behavior. I hope each of you will make decisions that will be the best ones for you. I will, of course, care for you and respect you at all times—even when there are problems—because I feel that this is the best way for teachers and students to get along together. I feel that, if we care for and respect each other, it will be best for all of us—best for you and best for me.

After the teacher finishes stating personal feelings and views, he should ask if there are any questions or comments. After he entertains all questions and comments, he may begin regularly scheduled tasks.

High school level strategies. On the first day, the high school teacher should begin by ensuring that pupils are in the right classroom. Immediately afterward, he might say:

I am Mr. Robinson, the homeroom teacher for grade . . . , section . . . . The first thing I would like to do today is to meet each of you individually. I am going to call the roll; when I call your name, hold up your hand; and, if you like, you may make a brief statement regarding your interests and what you want to accomplish this year. If you don't have any comments to make, however, please do not feel compelled to do so. [The teacher calls the roll and listens to students tell about their interests.]

There are two additional things I would like to do during this period. First, I would like to share with you some of my interests; and second, I would like to share some of my feelings with you. [The teacher spends a few minutes talking about personal academic interests.]

At this point, I'd like to share some of my feelings. I am of the opinion that students and teachers function best when they care for and respect each other. I believe this, and so I care for and respect each of you individually. Moreover, my caring for and respecting you is unconditional and will be maintained at all times—when things are going well and even when we have difficulties.

I would also like to say that each of you will be expected to perform and behave in a given fashion, a fashion determined by school administrative personnel and me. Each of you, however, will have to determine whether or not you will perform according to these expectations, and, of course, each of you will have to assume responsibility for your actions.

After the teacher has expressed his feelings and views, he should ask for questions and comments from class members. Following the discussion, regularly scheduled tasks may begin.

Seven secrets. Berne (1985) reveals seven "secrets," derived from seven self-esteem principles, she feels teachers can use to build the self-esteem of their pupils. She recommends that teachers:

1. Build in success: To ensure success, teachers should structure tasks into series of easy steps to minimize the probability of failure.

   The self-esteem principle associated with this recommendation is that, "Success builds self-esteem, especially when the chain of successes remains continuous and unbroken."

2. State the positive: Teachers should emphasize the positive aspects of their pupils' behavior and transmit information in a nonjudgmental fashion by describing and affirming rather than by judging.

   This follows the principle, "Acknowledging the positive in a nonevaluative but validating way, nurtures success."

3. Capitalize on successes: Teachers who capitalize on successes go further than merely capitalizing on interests. Thus, when interests have fostered successes, they go a step further and use these successful experiences to create new successes and expand pupils' interests.

   This is derived from the self-esteem principle that says, "Children will feel success is possible if you can help them build a history of similar successes."

4. Watch for sparks of growth: When a child develops

a keen interest or "spark" in a given area, provide him or her with encouragement and support. Teachers should use these sparks to assist pupils in developing new skills and learning how to relate to and interact more effectively with others.

This comes from the self-esteem principle that holds, "Children with low self-esteem tend to believe they cannot grow, learn, or successfully relate to other people. And, often, they won't—until a spark of interest is ignited."

5. Value and acknowledge: Teachers should acknowledge their students' accomplishments and communicate to them that they value their efforts and contributions.

This is from the principle, "Evidence of success that is visible and tangible has a strong positive effect on a child's self-esteem."

6. Keep expectations realistic: The expectations that teachers establish for their pupils should be appropriate for their ability, aptitude, and interest. Expectations should be neither too low nor too high, and students need to be treated as partners in the development of skills.

This follows the self-esteem principle, "Clearly stating reasonable expectations will help children with low self-esteem feel less anxious about pleasing others."

7. Don't be boring: Teachers should strive to make their classes and the subject matter they teach as exciting as possible. When children find learning exciting, they tend to learn more effectively.

The principle underlying this recommendation is, "Boredom depresses self-esteem; interest and excitement increase a sense of self. Active involvement in life nourishes self-esteem."

We recommend that the strategies just reviewed serve as models, and that teachers adopt terminology which is most effective for them in their unique situations as they attempt to establish positive interactive relationships with their pupils.

In their interactions with their pupils, teachers—like parents—can provide for them mutual respect, unconditional positive regard, encouragement, and enforced limits.

Psychotherapists

If parents and teachers are not successful in their own attempts to heighten the self-esteem of children in their care, the intervention of a psychotherapist is in order.

The effective psychotherapist interacts with the child in a nonjudgmental fashion and provides mutual respect and unconditional positive regard. The therapist also encourages the child, and uses techniques such as reflective listening in his or her attempts to assist the child in developing more positive perceptions of self-worth. The major role of the psychotherapist is to function as a teacher, specializing in the psychology of human dynamics.

As an effective teacher, the therapist communicates to his client that he possesses knowledge that he will give to the child, his client. This knowledge, the therapist lets the child know, will assist him in perceiving more accurately and behaving more effectively. Thus, the therapist interacts with the patient or client in a fashion that enables that person to develop his potential most efficiently. Effective therapists:

1. Instruct or teach their clients effective ways of perceiving.
2. Assist their clients in gaining greater insights regarding the etiology (or cause) of their behavior.
3. Teach their clients strategies for identifying and clarifying problem situations effectively.
4. Instruct their clients in modes of behaving that are self-enhancing rather than self-defeating.
5. Teach their clients effective strategies for exploring alternatives.

In the next few pages, we will look again at three of the case studies originally presented in Chapter 3—Harold, Bambi, and Bobby—to see the results of therapy for disordered self-esteem.

These clients, and others who will be described in following chapters, were all exposed to a psychotherapeutic approach I call the Rational-Eclectic Approach (Battle 1985). This approach is basically the same as Ellis' Rational-Emotive Approach; but we use aspects of other theoretical orientations (e.g., client-centered, socio-cultural, behavioral, psychoanalytic) that are less directive, place greater importance on the aspects of early interactions between parent and child, on the acquisition of insight, and on the proces of defense. The approach is comprised of the following steps:

Step 1, assessment and historical review: The patient is administered a number of personality inventories in an attempt to gather relevant data regarding his or her current modes of functioning. Patient expectations are assessed and therapeutic goals are established. A brief homework assignment is provided.

Step 2, interpretation of results: At this step, results earned on measures of personality are interpreted to the patient. A brief review of the major tenents of the rational-eclectic point of view is provided, and the patient is again provided a homework assignment.

Step 3, identification of irrational premises and self-defeating patterns. Irrational and illogical ideas possessed by the patient are identified, and the patient is shown why these ideas "don't work well." Self-defeating patterns are identified. Again, the patient is given a homework assignment.

Step 4, exploration of irrational premises and self-defeating patterns: Irrational dispositions and self-defeating patterns are attacked directly, and the patient is made aware of the probable consequences of these actions. Again, there is homework for the patient.

Step 5, introduction of adaptive forms of behavior: Alternative modes of behavior are discussed, and the patient is shown how to function more effectively. Again, homework.

Step 6, rehearsal of newly acquired modes of behavior: The patient at this point practices responding in a more rational fashion under the guidance of the therapist in the therapeutic environment. More homework.

Step 7, generalization of newly acquired skills into the general social milieu: The patient is shown how to take the skills learned in therapy and apply them in the real world. As usual, there is homework.

Step 8, review and follow-up: A review of the progress that has been made in therapy and elsewhere is conducted. The patient is encouraged to continually practice the newly developed skills and to assign homework to himself as often as he feels it is needed.

Case Report 4:1. Harold D.; 9 years, 9 months.
Results of therapy.

After six weeks of therapy involving Harold and his parents, Harold was able to resolve his major emotional problem and view himself in a more positive fashion. For instance, when he entered therapy he felt that his parents loved his sister but did not care for him. He was able to resolve this conflict in six weeks, but he continued to experience academic difficulties. Testing at this time indicated that Harold was not depressed and that his self-esteem had increased significantly. His self-esteem scores at that time were as follows:

Score

	Possible	Mean	Actual	%-ile	t	Class.
Total	50	35.7	36	48	51	inter.
General	20	14.2	19	96	65	v. high
Social	10	7.1	9	95	64	v. high
Academic	10	7.0	1	2	27	v. low
Parental	10	7.4	7	47	51	high

Case Report 4:2. Bambi J.; 14 years, 10 months.
Results of therapy.

During therapy, Bambi made significant gains. At the end of eight weeks, Bambi was not depressed. Her self-esteem scores were as follows:

Score

	Possible	Mean	Actual	%-ile	t	Class.
Total	32	23.7	27	78	58	high
General	16	12.0	12	58	53	high
Social	8	6.9	8	78	59	v. high
Personal	8	4.9	7	95	65	high

Case Report 4:3. Bobby B.; 28 years, married.
Results of therapy.

. After ten weeks of therapy, Bobby was able to resolve his emotional difficulties and modify his self-defeating patterns. Testing at this time indicated that Bobby was not depressed and that his self-esteem had increased significantly. His scores were as follows:

. . . .

		Score				
	Possible	Mean	Actual	%-ile	*t*	Class.
Total	32	23.7	27	75	58	high
General	16	12.0	13	71	57	high
Social	8	6.9	7	80	60	high
Personal	8	4.9	7	90	63	high

. . . .

Bobby was able to gain readmission to the university on this occasion, and was able to maintain an average of 80 percent in his classes. He completed university training two years later. He is currently successfully employed in an important administrative position.

SUMMARY

1. Children experiencing disordered self-esteem require remediation.
2. Three important sources of remediation for children experiencing disordered self-esteem are parents, teachers, and psychotherapists.
3. Parents should provide for their children enforced limits, encouragement, and unconditional positive regard.
4. Once the child enters school, teachers function "in loco parentis," and as a consequence inherit the ability to influence significantly the self-esteem of their pupils.

III

ENHANCING SELF-ESTEEM

Chapter 5

STRATEGIES FOR ENHANCING SELF-ESTEEM

It is important that we attend to the self-esteem needs of developing children and youth, because self-esteem is the most important variable affecting the lives of all of us. Branden states that self-esteem is a fundamental need of humans that should not be neglected, because—if humans fail to acquire a significant degree of self-esteem—they will strive to "fake it" and display pseudo-self-esteem, an irrational, self-protective device designed to reduce anxiety and enhance a sense of security (1969). I myself have stated elsewhere that self-esteem affects one's level of achievement, ability to adjust to environmental demands, and general state of well-being.

Enhancment of self-esteem, as I propose it, is a growth-oriented process which is based on the premise that all children can improve their ability to develop their potential most effectively. Thus, the process of enhancing self-esteem should be a goal for all children, whether they possess low, intermediate, or high self-esteem. Enhancing self-esteem is not just for children experiencing disordered self-esteem; rather, it is for all children.

Self-esteem is not a unitary phenomenon; rather, it is

multifaceted. Thus, enhancement strategies should be fairly specialized, designed to enhance specific facets of self-esteem. The strategies of enhancement listed in this chapter are specifically intended to enhance the four major facets of self-esteem: (1) general self-esteem, (2) social self-esteem, (3) academic self-esteem, and (4) parent-related self-esteem.

Enhancing General Self-Esteem

General self-esteem is the aspect of self-esteem which refers to an individual's overall general perceptions of his worth. Strategies that have proven to be effective in enhancing general self-esteem include: (a) self-image enhancement programs, (b) individual counseling, and (c) group counseling.

Self-image enhancement programs. Mettee, Williams, and Reed (1972) found that a self-image enhancement program which involved tutoring and self-image enhancement sessions induced positive shifts in the self-esteem of 58 subjects ages seven to ten who received tutoring from undergraduate university students for a five-month period.

Individual counseling. Individual counseling is an idiographic procedure in which two individuals, therapist and client, interact in an attempt to assist the client in resolving the problems he or she is experiencing.

Group counseling. In group counseling, two or more individuals (usually four to 12) interact with a therapist in an attempt to assist each member of the group in resolving the problems each is experiencing. Group counseling, unlike individual counseling, provides the opportunity for interchange of several points of view and permits a large amount of feedback for each participating member.

Enhancing Social Self-Esteem

Social self-esteem is the aspect of self-esteem that refers to the individual's perceptions of interpersonal peer relationships. Strategies that have proved to be effective in this realm include: (a) individual counseling, (b) group counseling, (c) class discussion, (d) the jigsaw puzzle technique, (e) school camping, (f) DUSO, and (g) Magic Circle programs.

Individual counseling. Individual counseling provides a private setting for the client, with the help of the therapist, to air and resolve problems of a social nature.

Group counseling. Group counseling offers a limited and structured forum—and a financially economical one, too—for resolution of problems, under the guidance of a professionally trained psychologist, psychiatrist, counselor, or social worker.

Class discussion. Class discussion is a group method which can be used to assist children and youth develop better interpersonal relationships. Class discussions can also be used to promote communication skills and facilitate the development of problem-solving abilities. In addition, class discussions provide opportunities for emotional and intellectual rehearsal, reassurance, and support, and chances to deal with specific problems of group members.

The jigsaw puzzle technique. This technique was developed by Aronson and colleagues, who felt it would promote cooperation and enhance the self-esteem of participating pupils. Aronson and his research group agrued that we should deemphasize competitiveness in our classrooms and encourage children to use one another as resources, rather than as competitors; they proposed that teachers should encourage cooperation and mutual respect, rather than competitiveness and opposition. To test their hypothesis, they studied children in Austin, Texas, for six weeks and found that:

1. Children in the jigsaw groups liked their peers more at the end of the six weeks than did children in the traditional classrooms.
2. Students in the jigsaw groups saw each other as learning resources; those in the traditional classrooms did not.
3. Children in the jigsaw groups had stronger and more positive self-concepts at the end of the experiment; their self-esteem improved; and they felt increasingly more important in school, than did children in the traditional classrooms.
4. Children in the jigsaw groups not only felt better about themselves and liked their classmates better;

they also generally appeared to be more accepting of themselves and others.

School camping. Some experts propose that school camping programs stimulate emotional growth and promote the development of initiative and self-determination in participants. In an attempt to test this hypothesis, Beker (1960) studied 261 sixth-grade subjects who participated in seven school encampments, and a comparable group of 96 controls who were pre- and posttested only. A summary of the findings of Beker's study is presented in Table 5:1.

TABLE 5:1. *Number of Items Showing Significant Shifts on the Self-Concept Checklist (N = 357).*

Shift	n	Boys	Girls	Both	No Shift
1st to 2nd Admin.					
Experimental	261	15+	11+	22+	23
Control	96	3+	3+	4+,1-	42
p		.01	.05	.001	.001
1st to 3rd Admin.					
Experimental	261	22+	19+	35+	11
Control	96	6+	4+	8+	36
p		.001	.001	.001	.001

Note 1: The difference from the second to the third administration shown by the experimental group was reliable at the .01 level for the number of items showing significant shifts by the entire group and for the number showing no significant shift. It was not reliable at the .05 level for either sex alone in the experimental group or for any of the four categories in the control group.

Note 2: The checklist consisted of 47 items. The rows total more than 47 because some items shifted in more than one of the three categories listed.

Source: Beker, J. 1960. The influence of school camping on the self-concepts and social relationships of sixth-grade children. *Journal of Educational Psychology* 51:352-356. Reprinted by permission.

Results shown in Table 5:1 indicate that campers experienced more positive shifts in perceptions of self-worth than their noncamping counterparts. In another study, Meston and I (1976) studied adolescent boys and found that a camping experience was effective in significantly enhancing the self-concepts of juvenile delinquents. Since then, of course, more information has come to light concerning the value of camping.

There are, for example, several wilderness survival programs being offered, especially in the western United States, designed specifically for delinquent youth, which have demonstrated success rates in improving the social adaptive behavior of their clients; and camping is a major part of the curriculum in many private and parochial schools.

Like the jigsaw technique, in which class projects are structured so that they can only be accomplished effectively when students cooperate with each other to reach goals and solve problems, successful camping requires participants to "pull together," sharing the responsibilities and the workload that all camping entails. The outdoors, furthermore, lends a sense of immediacy and realism to work performed. For example, the group may not be able to have dinner until the firewood has been gathered and split, the fire laid properly, matches or striker have been available to light it, and the food and utensils are ready. The powerful nature of the camping experience is nowhere more obvious than in the newspaper reports seen from time to time, when some disaster in the woods has been averted or ameliorated by resourcefulness and cooperation of those in danger.

DUSO. Developing Understanding of Self and Others (DUSO) is a program of activities and materials designed to help children of preschool and early primary age understand social and emotional behavior. The DUSO program encourages children to develop positive self-images, to become more aware of the relationship between themselves and others, and to recognize their own personal needs and goals.

The DUSO program is based on the assumptions that:

1. Children's social and emotional needs are related to their academic needs. One can assume that the development of an understanding of self and others is central to a complete educational process.

2. Learning is fostered by an environment that builds a child's positive self-concept and feelings of acceptance and belonging.
3. Children can learn to talk about their own feelings and the feelings of others.
4. Children can learn by talking with others about feelings, goals, and behavior.
5. Children can learn that feelings, goals, and behavior are dynamically related (Dinkmeyer and Dinkmeyer (1982, p. 7).

The activities incorporated in the DUSO program are organized into three units: developing understanding of self, developing understanding of others, and developing understanding of choices.

Magic Circle. Magic Circle is a human development program which was designed to assist children in developing their personal effectiveness, self-confidence, and understanding of the causes and effects in interpersonal relationships. Magic Circle is a preventive program intended to help children understand and respect themselves and others. The basic assumptions incorporated in the Magic Circle program are:

1. The inherent worth of every individual.
2. The right of each person to be self-determining.
3. The right and need of each person to have acceptance and affection.

Enhancing Academic Self-Esteem

Academic (school-related) self-esteem is the aspect of self-esteem that refers to the individual's perception of his ability to succeed academically. Programs and strategies that have proven to be effective in this area include: (a) parent training programs, (b) youth-tutoring-youth programs, (c) partially integrated mainstreaming, and (d) teacher-pupil interactions.

Parent training programs. A number of experts have used parent training programs to enhance the self-esteem and academic achievement levels of children of participating parents. In a well known study, Brookover et al. (1965) employed parents to exert positive shifts on their children's self-perceptions and perception of ability. In the study, researchers met with parents for a one-year period and discussed with them a variety of topics intended to assist the parents in their attempts to help their children develop more effectively. Brookover and his colleagues found that parents who participated in group sessions were able to induce significant positive shifts in their children's self-perceptions and perception of ability to achieve academically.

Youth-tutoring-youth programs. Youth-tutoring-youth programs have been used effectively to enhance academic self-esteem and achievement levels. Although youth-tutoring-youth is a well established technique, it has only recently been employed in a systematic fashion. Also, only recently have we used these programs to assist both tutors and tutees. Results derived from a variety of studies indicate that tutors usually benefit as much as tutees from the tutoring experience (Frager and Stern 1970; Allen and Feldman 1972).

In addition to enhancement of academic self-esteem and achievement levels, tutors usually experience other benefits. For instance, several researchers have reported that tutors generally experience improvement in motivation, sense of responsibility, self-esteem, and in attitudes toward school.

Partially integrated mainstreaming. Partially integrated mainstreaming has been used effectively to enhance the self-esteem of children experiencing learning problems. In this type of program, children receive instruction in areas in which they are deficient, in self-contained special education classes, but are integrated in the mainstream for all other classes. Research findings indicate that partially integrated mainstreaming enhances the self-esteem of participating students. For instance, Andriashek and I (1980) studied learning-disabled children ages eight through 12 who had been placed in special education programs because they were experiencing academic deficits of two years or more in reading and arithmetic. These students were randomly assigned two groups: (1) those who were partially integrated into regular classes for a portion of the school day (experimental group), and (2) those who remained in self-contained special education classes for the entire school day (control group). Experimental subjects were integrated into regular classes for science, music, health, and physical education, but received instruction in reading and arithmetic in self-contained special education classrooms. Findings of our study, displayed in Table 5:2, indicate that subjects who were partially integrated experienced significantly higher gains in self-esteem than those who were not partially integrated. Findings of the study indicate that mainstreaming of special education students experiencing learning deficits for part of the school day is an effective way of bolstering their self-esteem.

TABLE 5:2. *Pre- and Posttest Means for Experimental and Control Groups.*

| | Experimental | | Control | |
	Pre	Post	Pre	Post
Total	31.5	33.7	37.1	33.5
General	13.0	14.1	14.9	13.7
Social	4.1	4.4	6.2	5.9
Academic	6.8	7.2	7.3	6.4
Parental	7.6	7.6	9.0	7.9

In another research project, Smith et al. (1977) studied special education students who were integrated for half a day with regular class students, along with a comparable group of special education students who received instruction in their self-contained special class for the entire school day. Findings of the study are summarized in Table 5:3.

Teacher-pupil interactions. The interaction between teacher and pupil is a major force affecting the academic self-esteem of students. I have said elsewhere (1981, 1982, 1983) that a positive teacher-pupil interactive process will enhance the self-esteem of pupils. If a child interacts with a teacher who establishes a positive teacher-pupil interactive process, the child will learn more and his academic self-esteem will be enhanced. Conversely, if the teacher does not establish a good relationship with the student, the child will learn less and, as a consequence, will not experience signi-

TABLE 5:3. *Means of Self-Concept of Participating Subjects.*

	Test 1	Test 2	Test 3
Control	53.08	55.32	55.20
Experimental	52.60	58.92	63.68

ficant gains in academic self-esteem.

The teacher-pupil interactive process is one in which the teacher communicates to the child that he is an individual who is worthy and significant—and that this evaluation is not contingent on any predetermined conditions. It is a process in which the teacher provides structure for the child, and communicates to him that he is expected to perform and behave in a certain fashion. It is also communicated to the child that he can determine whether or not he will function in the expected fashion, and that he will have to assume the responsibility for his actions.

Other experts also propose that how teachers interact with their pupils exerts a strong effect on their pupils' self-esteem. For instance, Staines (1958) studied the interactions between teachers and pupils, and found that teachers who interacted positively with their pupils induced positive changes in their students' self-esteem; whereas teachers who did not interact positively with their pupils induced negative shifts in the self-esteem of their pupils.

Both perceived academic success (perception of ability) and actual academic success (usually presented in grades or stanines) are affected by the interactions between teacher and pupil. Students' perception of their ability to perform academic tasks, and their actual performance on these tasks, affect academic self-esteem. For instance, Yaniw (1983) studied 716 junior high school boys and girls and found that academic self-esteem correlated significantly with both perceived academic success and actual academic success. Findings of Yaniw's study are presented in Table 5:4.

The data displayed in Table 5:4 clearly indicate that academic self-esteem is more closely related to perceived and actual academic success than other facets of self-esteem.

TABLE 5:4. *Correlations of Self-Esteem with Academic Achievement (N = 716).*

| | Year-End Final Grades | | | |
	Math	Lang. Arts	Social S.	Science
Total	.33***	.38***	.37***	.38***
General	.17***	.21***	.20***	.22***
Social	.07*	.11**	.06*	.05
Academic	.57***	.59***	.61***	.60***
Parental	.19***	.21***	.23***	.25***

*p = .05   **p = .01   ***p = .001

The same patterns are evident in findings of Yaniw's study delineating the relationship between self-esteem and achievement in mathematics, language arts, social studies, and science.

Summaries of these findings are presented in Tables 5:5 through 5:8, respectively.

TABLE 5.5. *Self-Esteem Means for Five Achievement Level Groups in Mathematics.*

| | | Year-End Final Grades (%) | | | | |
	Pos. Score	80-100	65-79	50-64	40-49	<40
Total	50	38.98	37.62	34.13	33.46	31.03
General	20	15.87	15.81	14.67	14.77	14.24
Social	10	7.38	7.38	7.01	7.18	7.07
Academic	10	7.72	6.63	5.26	4.35	3.36
Parental	10	7.94	7.66	7.18	7.15	6.23
	N =	161	187	200	93	75

TABLE 5:6. *Self-Esteem Means for Five Achievement Level Groups in Language Arts.*

Year-End Final Grades (%)

	Pos. Score	80-100	65-79	50-64	40-49	<40
Total	50	39.73	37.79	34.86	30.95	29.09
General	20	15.76	15.89	15.07	13.96	13.00
Social	10	7.52	7.33	7.23	6.73	6.82
Academic	10	8.35	6.74	5.16	3.83	3.41
Parental	10	7.97	7.76	7.32	6.44	5.85
N =		89	248	256	89	34

TABLE 5.7. *Self-Esteem Means for Five Achievement Level Groups in Social Studies.*

Year-End Final Grades (%)

	Pos. Score	80-100	65-79	50-64	40-49	<40
Total	50	40.00	38.03	35.05	31.38	31.45
General	20	15.86	15.94	15.18	13.85	14.33
Social	10	7.47	7.34	7.07	7.13	7.08
Academic	10	8.20	7.03	5.26	4.03	3.48
Parental	10	8.35	7.59	7.50	6.38	6.52
N =		104	215	212	125	60

Enhancing Parent-Related Self-Esteem

Parent-related (home-related) self-esteem is the aspect of self-esteem that refers to the individual's perception of his status at home—which includes his subjective perceptions of how his parents view him. Strategies that have been used effectively to enhance parent-related self-esteem include (a) counseling, and (b) parent-child interaction.

Counseling. Counseling can be used effectively to

TABLE 5:8. *Self-Esteem Means for Five Achievement Level Groups in Science.*

| | Pos. Score | Year-End Final Grades (%) | | | | |
		80-100	65-79	50-64	40-49	<40
Total	50	39.94	37.89	34.92	32.21	30.23
General	20	15.99	15.92	15.09	13.97	14.08
Social	10	7.37	7.37	7.04	7.22	7.26
Academic	10	8.22	6.80	5.39	4.16	3.24
Parental	10	8.24	7.69	7.34	6.84	5.64
	$N =$	110	187	261	105	53

facilitate this area of self-esteem if both parents and child are willing to participate, and if parents are flexible enough to change. If parents are willing to modify the way that they are communicating with and interacting with their child, it will exert a positive effect on the child's perception of his relationship with his parents.

In the counseling process, parents should work cooperatively with a professionally trained therapist who should teach them more effective ways of dealing with their children. In addition, the therapist should teach parents how to assist their children in clarifying problems more precisely, exploring alternatives and choosing modes of behaving that are self-enhancing rather than self-defeating.

Parent-child interaction. The parent-child interactive process is the most powerful, important variable affecting their children's self-esteem.

Interaction is a complex process that incorporates both verbal and nonverbal components. Although these two components are highly interrelated, they do not necessarily work in synchrony. What a person says does not necessarily communicate to the receiving individual that the statement accurately represents what the person feels and perceives. Thus, the nonverbal aspect of the communication process may be incongruent with the verbal aspect. Simply because the parent says to the child that she loves him, it does not mean that the child will feel that he is loved. For example, in an interview I conducted with a parent and her nine-year-old son, the mother stated, "I don't know why Billy has so many problems; he knows we all love him." The boy replied, "The teachers at school love me, but you and Dad don't." The child was subsequently referred to a psychiatrist, who agreed that the parents did not love the boy, and who recommended that he be taken into custody by the social service department and be removed from his parents' home.

Because the interactions between parent and child are so crucial to the well-being of the child, it is essential that parents make overt attempts to provide their children mutual respect, unconditional positive regard, and encouragement.

      .   .   .   .   .

The strategies just listed have proven to be effective in enhancing various facets of self-esteem.

The reader, however, should note that, although a specific strategy may be designed to enhance a given facet of self-esteem, its effects are not limited to that one facet. For instance, activities intended to enhance or promote academic self-esteem may have a generalizing effect, and as a consequence enhance general and social self-esteem as well.

The following case reports are presented to illustrate how the various facets of self-esteem can be promoted. Although all facets of self-esteem are enhanced in most cases, the present examples have been selected on the basis of the relative "weight" assigned to one or another of four major self-esteem areas.

Case Report 5:1. Rene J.; 12 years.
Low self-esteem and underachievement.

Rene was the youngest in a family of three children. He was the only boy, with sisters ages 13 and 15. His mother stated that the pregnancy, birth process, and early developmental history were normal. Rene walked at 12 months, started to use sentences at 16 months, and was toilet trained at 3 years, 1 month.

Rene's mother noted that his problems started when he first entered kindergarten. In kindergarten, he experienced "separation anxiety" and cried constantly when his mother attempted to leave the classroom. His mother unfortunately decided to sit outside the door of the classroom to assure Rene that she would be there if he needed her. When the half-day kindergarten class was over, Rene's mother would walk him home. This procedure continued for the first four weeks of kindergarten. After this period, Rene reluctantly agreed to stay in school alone, but insisted that his mother walk him home after the school day was over. This persistence on the part of Rene prevailed when he entered first grade. In addition, he tended to be shy; he rarely "mixed" with other children; and on the few occasions he did play with other children, his profound egocentricity strained social relations. Other children tended to avoid him.

Rene experienced severe learning problems throughout his elementary years, and was diagnosed as being a child with a "learning disability due to dyslexia." Each year, teachers recommended that he repeat his grade, but his parents insisted that he be promoted because they were afraid that failure would have a negative effect on his self-esteem.

When Rene was in eighth grade, his mother became involved in the local chapter of the association for parents of children with learning disabilities. It was through her involvement with this organization that she attended a workshop dealing with learning disabilities. She subsequently contacted a psychologist and requested that he interview Rene. He assessed Rene as being a bright child who was underachieving. He was not dyslexic, and there were no indications of biological dysfunction. Rene was experiencing severe academic deficits, basically, because he had refused to cooperate and use his potential effectively.

The psychologist recommended that the parents provide more structure at home for the client. He also recommended that Rene receive individual tutoring in reading, spelling, and arithmetic. In addition, Rene received counseling designed to enhance self-esteem and make him aware of his self-defeating patterns and of the probable consequences of such actions. Rene's pre- and posttest scores are reported here:

Test	Grade Score June 1979	Grade Score July 1980	Grade Score August 1980
Schonell Reading	4.5	5.8	6.1
Schonell Spelling	3.5	5.2	5.6
Schonell Comp.	4.5	8.0	9.3
Bett's Vocab.	4.5	6.0	6.2
Monroe-Sherman	5.5	5.9	10.0

Self-Esteem	Score	Score	Score
Total	24	31	34
General	9	13	15
Social	4	6	7
Academic	3	4	4
Parental	8	8	8

Case Report 5:2. Robert B.; 9 years, 6 months.
Low social self-esteem.

Robert was the oldest child in a family of three children. His mother reported that the pregnancy and birth process were normal, and that development during the first four years was generally normal. Robert walked at 9 months, started to use sentences at 18 months, and was toilet trained at 2 years, 6 months.

Robert attended nursery school when he was three and a half, and enrolled in a bilingual (French-English) kindergarten when he was four and a half. Robert experienced some minor problems in this setting, but his major difficulties were in his interpersonal interactions with peers. Robert was transferred into a standard public school during his second year. In this setting, he made rapid academic progress but continued to have difficulties with peers.

At this point, Robert was referred to me. I found him to be a bright, highly egocentric child who possessed very poor interpersonal skills. Robert's Verbal, Performance, and Full Scale IQ scores from the WISC-R were 124, 129, and 129 respectively. Self-esteem results indicate that Robert possessed average to above-average self-esteem in all facets except the social one, which was very low. Analysis of his self-esteem scores revealed the following:

. . . .

		Score			
	Possible	Mean	Actual	%-ile	t	Class.
General	20	14.2	12	31	46	inter.
Social	10	7.1	2	7	33	v. low
Academic	10	7.0	7	61	54	high
Parental	10	7.4	9	87	61	high

. . . .

After eight weeks of therapy with Robert and his parents, he became less egocentric, and was able to develop his interpersonal skills more effectively. Testing on this occasion revealed the following self-esteem profile:

. . . .

		Score			
	Possible	Mean	Actual	%-ile	t	Class.
General	20	14.2	20	96	65	v. high
Social	10	7.1	9	95	64	v. high
Academic	10	7.0	10	91	63	v. high
Parental	10	7.4	10	87	61	v. high

. . . .

Case Report 5:3. Homer J.; 9 years, 3 months.
Low self-esteem and learning disability.

Homer was the eldest of three children in a family. His mother reported that the pregnancy and initial phases of the birth process were uneventful; but labor was long (approximately 18 hours); and high forceps had to be used to deliver the child. Forceps-delivery did not create any visible scars, but the attending physician told the mother that the subject was "a fathead baby." Homer weighed 8 pounds at birth and was a difficult and active child from the outset. He was "overly active," yelled and screamed frequently, did not sleep well, and did not enjoy being held or cuddled. Some other aspects of development, however, were positive. For instance, Homer was sitting up at 6 months, walking at 8 months, and starting to use sentences at 18 months. Nevertheless, he continued to present problems for his parents. He found it very difficult to sit still, was constantly on the run, got into everything, climbed on tables, dressers, the stove, and the refrigerator.

In an attempt to keep him "pinned down" for brief periods of time, Homer's parents would chain his bedroom door, so he couldn't get out and disrupt things. Homer started to "bang" his head and "rock" when he was age 2. His head-banging behavior ceased, but he remained a "rocker." He was toilet trained at 2 years, 6 months, but continued to be enuretic, so that his physician placed him on Tofranil for this problem when he was 8.

When Homer was three years old, he ran a temperature of 105° — which his parents unsuccessfully tried to reduce by administering aspirin and giving him sponge baths. He experienced a febrile convulsion which resulted in unconsciousness for a 20-minute period. He was hospitalized the next day, and was administered an EEG which revealed slight abnormalities. His physician prescribed phenobarbital for this condition. Subsequent EEG findings approximately two years later were normal, and the phenobarbital was discontinued.

After the seizure, Homer was particularly susceptible to fevers, colds, and allergies. His sleep also became more disturbed. Often, approximately twice a week, he woke up during the night, ran to his parents' bedroom, terrified, crying for help. On the mornings after these episodes, Homer had no recollection of them. His parents assumed that he was having nightmares. Homer's mother also reported that, on occasion, Homer would become "beside himself," lash out, cry, throw and break things. When these episodes occurred, she would give him 5 mg of Valium and put him to bed. Homer's activity level also increased after his seizure, so his physician prescribed methylphenidate (Ritalin) for his "hyperactivity." The Ritalin, however, was not effective in curtailing the "hyperactivity," so that medication was abandoned in favor of Dilantin.

Homer was examined by a neurologist when he was nine years old; this physician concluded that Homer's problems could be attributed to a difficult birth. He also reported that he was of the opinion that his patient had a low threshold for seizures, and that he might be an arrested hydrocephalic. He predicted that Homer would not be able to complete a regular fourth-grade program, and recommended that he be considered as a candidate for a special education program.

Homer was also examined by an opthalmologist during his ninth year, who reported that his client did not have any perceptual, neurological, or motor difficulties. The opthalmologist concluded that Homer did not have a "learning disability," and that his problem was basically psychological in nature. About this time, Homer was also seen by a psychologist, who provided psychotherapy for him. The psychologist concluded that Homer was making poor academic progress because he possessed a negative "self-concept."

Homer's mother and father were 22 and 24 years old respectively when he was born. His mother is a nurse and his father is a businessman. Both parents have generally experienced good health, but the family history is positive for neurological disease. The mother has a cousin who is epileptic, and the father's two sisters have children with neurological deficits in the form of meningocele and a cerebral vascular accident. The father reported that he was treated for a nocturnal seizure several years ago. He was administered an EEG at the time and findings were abnormal, but no specific treatment was prescribed. Since then, however, he has not experienced any similar symptoms or difficulties; nor had he had any problems prior to the episode. The mother had an EEG administered to her because she felt that there might be "genetic" causes for Homer's problems, but no abnormalities were noted.

The school psychologist and reading specialist assessed Homer, met with parents and school officials, and interpreted results. The parents informed the members of the group of the many difficulties Homer had experienced since birth, and advised them that they had reached "the end." They stated that they were totally frustrated and had finally accepted the reality that their child would not be successful in a regular class program. Thus, they were willing to have Homer placed in a special education program, and had made tentative arrangements for him to be placed in a special school for autistic and learning-disabled children. The specialists advised the parents that the public school system had its own special classes for children with learning disabilities and that—if they liked— arrangements could be made to have Homer placed in one of these classes.

The parents agreed to such a placement, and requested that it be initiated as soon as possible. The specialists, however, did recommend that Homer be referred for one more additional set of assessments prior to placement. The parents were somewhat reluctant to have additional assessments, but nevertheless agreed to follow up on the recommendations.

Homer, thus, was seen by a neuropsychologist who uses computer-powered spectral EEG analyses in addition to traditional neuropsychological procedures. The neuropsychological profile derived from these tests indicated that Homer was experiencing mild to moderate bilateral dysfunction in both cerebral hemispheres. The dysfunction was primarily localized in the anterior regions of the brain, with the localization of the dysfunction being different for the two hemispheres. The left hemisphere dysfunction was found primarily in the posterior frontal and left temporal regions; whereas the right hemisphere dysfunction was found more in the anterior prefrontal and temporal regions. The computerized EEG analyses revealed abnormal, excessive fast frequency activity in the left temporal region (T_3) and the right prefrontal (Fp_2) and parietal (P_4) regions. There was also evidence for excess activity in the right temporal regions for three of the seven situations, and Homer did not manifest normal suppression of EEG activity under task control for the left posterior frontal (F_7) and temporal (T_3) regions and the right prefrontal (Fp_2) and parietal (P_4) regions. The neuropsychologist concluded that the episodic violent outbursts, absences, and visual and tactile hallucinations were due to active epilepsy. He interviewed the parents, interpreted his findings, and recommended that Homer be seen by a neurologist for a 16-channel EEG. Results from the EEG administered by the neurologist indicated a generalized dysrhythmia mostly over the left hemisphere. The neurologist concluded that Homer's problem was probably due to a minimal brain damage (MBD) syndrome which was possibly associated with his fibrile disorder and convulsion when he was three years old . . . or perhaps related to a difficult birth. He continued by stating that the brain damage seemed to be manifested by Homer's personality problems and possibly dysgraphia and dyslexia as well.

The people primarily responsible for providing treatment for Homer were two teachers and a child psychiatrist. The school psychologist and reading specialist functioned as consultants in the case, and conferred with the psychiatrist, teachers, and parents throughout the treatment process. They also made recommendations concerning specific programming and behavior management. The consultants, for instance, recommended to school officials that Homer be placed in the school's resource room program. (The resource room is a small-group, tutorial-type support class intended to assist students in reading and arithmetic. The class is staffed by a certified teacher trained in remedial techniques; typically, there are only three to five students in the class at any given time. Resource room participants remain in the regular class program, but spend several hours a week in the resource room receiving assistance in reading and arithmetic.)

Specialists also recommended to Homer's teachers that they:

— Expose Homer to a structured program that emphasizes both oral and written skills.
— Clarify expectations thoroughly and provide instructions in short, concise sequences.
— Attempt to aid the development of attentional skills by rewarding Homer accordingly (e.g., permission to participate in self-selected activities, or offering verbal praise) when he attends appropriately.
— Encourage Homer to read aloud to his class, starting with easy material and increasing the complexity gradually to ensure success and avoid failure.
— Emphasize Homer's positive, rather than negative, qualities. Create learning experiences that are success oriented, and reprimand him only when absolutely necessary. (In instances deemed worthy of reprimand, it should be done as privately and quietly as possible.)

The resource room teacher's initial impressions of Homer were extremely negative. She felt that he possessed a defeatist attitude and demonstrated considerable lack of confidence. She stated that he tended to withdraw when he felt "pressured," rarely volunteered answers in class, and displayed apprehensiveness when he felt she would call on him to answer questions. She also reported that Homer appeared to be nervous and "unsure" of himself, that he frequently manifested psychosomatic symptoms (e.g., twitching), and occasionally displayed "outbursts" of tears and hostility. When this would happen, Homer would remove himself from the classroom and sit until he "recollected" himself. She described Homer as being a poor sportsman who would quit in the middle of a game if he felt he was losing. In addition, Homer experienced considerable interpersonal difficulties with peers, and found it extremely difficult to establish eye-to-eye contact with them. Academically, he was weak in language arts, and especially weak in spelling.

Homer's regular classroom teacher described him in the following fashion: "Homer has a very poor self-concept. He gives up easily and hopes that he will not be forced to try. He is very nervous, twitches constantly, and 'turns off' whenever he decides to quit trying. He is easily discouraged with paperwork."

The child psychiatrist placed Homer on Tegretol (300 mg daily) initially; but teacher reports indicated that it induced drowsiness at school. The doctor therefore subsequently placed Homer on pertofrane (50 mg daily)—which, to this date, appears to be working effectively.

When last observed, Homer was sleeping nights; he was alert and attentive at school; behavioral difficulties had diminished both at home and at school; and he was making satisfactory academic progress. Homer's standardized test score results over a two-year period were as follows:

Subject Area	Grade Score June 1976	Grade Score June 1977	Grade Score June 1978
Reading	1.3	2.7	5.0
Accuracy	1.7	4.6	5.1
Comprehension	1.6	4.1	5.1
Spelling	2.0	2.5	3.8
Arithmetic	2.4	3.8	5.0
IQ (WISC-R)	98	100	106

Self-Esteem	Score	Score	Score
Total	20	33	38
General	8	10	12
Social	4	8	8
Academic	0	7	9
Parental	8	8	9

Case Report 5:4. Sarah H.; 10 years, 7 months.
Low parental self-esteem, learning disability, and
depression.

Sarah was the elder of two children in a family. Her mother reported that the pregnancy and birth process went smoothly, and that development during the early years was generally normal. Sarah started to walk at 12 months, was toilet trained at 22 months, and started to use sentences when she was 2.

Sarah enrolled in kindergarten with her age-peers. Her achievement was normal during that time, but she had severe academic deficits the year following, so she repeated first grade. This did not resolve her academic problems, because she continued to have learning difficulties in second, third, and fourth grade. During the latter part of fourth grade, Sarah was referred to a psychologist who diagnosed her as being a learning-disabled child who was depressed and possessed low self-esteem. Her WISC-R Verbal, Performance, and Full Scale IQ scores were 88, 102, and 94 respectively. Her self-esteem scores were as follows:

	Score					
	Possible	Mean	Actual	%-ile	t	Class.
Total	50	35.7	20	5	33	low
General	20	14.2	10	23	43	inter.
Social	10	7.1	1	7	33	v. low
Academic	10	7.0	5	43	43	inter.
Parental	10	7.4	4	35	35	low

When psychotherapy commenced, Sarah was experiencing considerable difficulties in her interactions with her mother and stepfather. Sarah and her younger brother had different natural fathers. Sarah felt that her mother and stepfather loved her brother, but did not care for her.

After nine weeks of therapy that included Sarah and her mother, Sarah was able to resolve her major emotional difficulties. During this same period, she was provided with individual tutoring in reading, spelling, and arithmetic—which enabled her to reduce her academic deficits and allow her to achieve, generally, at grade level. Testing at this time indicated that Sarah was not depressed and that her self-esteem had increased significantly. Her self-esteem scores were as follows:

. . . .

Score

	Possible	Mean	Actual	%-ile	t	Class.
Total	50	35.7	27	18	41	inter.
General	20	14.2	13	45	50	inter.
Social	10	7.1	2	12	37	v. low
Academic	10	7.0	4	13	38	low
Parental	10	7.4	8	60	55	high

. . . .

SUMMARY

1. Self-esteem affects one's level of achievement, ability to adjust to environmental demands, and general state of well-being.
2. The enhancement of self-esteem is a growth-oriented process which should be a goal for all children.
3. Because self-esteem is multifaceted, enhancement strategies should be specialized, designed to enhance specific facets of self-esteem.
4. Although a specific strategy may be designed to enhance a given facet of self-esteem, its effects are not limited to the one facet. Generalization may occur, so that it affects other facets of self-esteem as well.

Chapter 6

ENHANCING THE SELF-ESTEEM
OF EXCEPTIONAL CHILDREN AND YOUTH

The strategies described in Chapter 5 generally exert a positive effect on all children; however, some exceptional children require more specialized forms of help in order for them to develop their potential more fully. In this chapter, therefore, we will describe enhancement techniques designed specifically for exceptional children which should be used *in conjunction with* the strategies from Chapter 5. The teaching techniques cited here are by no means exhaustive; but they offer a worthwhile "jumping-off point" as teachers and parents develop their own programs.

Exceptional children who require specialized forms of enhancement include: (1) the learning disabled, (2) the gifted, (3) the emotionally disordered, (4) the behaviorally disordered, and (5) the troubled and unemployed youth.

The Learning-Disabled Child

Experts differ at both conceptual and operational levels regarding what a learning disability is. Consequently, definitions regarding what a learning disability is, vary. A commonly quoted definition is the one offered by Hobbs (1975), in which he states that the learning disabled are:

> . . . Those children of any age who demonstrate a substantial deficiency in a particular aspect of academic achievement because of perceptual or perceptual-motor handicaps, regardless of etiology or other contributing factors. The term perceptual as used here relates to those mental (neurological) processes through which the child acquires his basic alphabets of sounds and forms. The term perceptual handicap refers to inadequate ability in such areas as the following: recognizing the differences between auditory and visual discriminating features underlying the sounds used in speech and the orthographic forms used in reading; retaining and recalling those discriminated sounds and forms sequentially both in short- and long-term memory; ordering the sounds and forms sequentially, both in short- and long-term memory; ordering the sounds and forms sequentially both in sensory and motor acts . . . ; distinguishing figure-ground relationships; recognizing spatial and temporal orientations; obtaining closure . . . ; integrating intersensory information . . . ; relating what is perceived to motor functions (p. 306).

Public Law 94-142, entitled "Education for All Handicapped Children," defines the learning disabled in the following fashion:

> Specific learning disability means a disorder in one or more of the basic psychological processes involved in understanding or in using language, spoken or written, which may manifest itself in an imperfect ability to listen, think, speak, read, write, spell, or do mathematical calculations. The term includes such conditions as perceptual handicap, brain injury, minimal brain dysfunction, dyslexia, and developmental aphasia. The term does not include children who have learning problems which are primarily the result of visual, hearing, or motor handicaps, or mental retardation, or of environmental, cultural, or economic disadvantage (Sect. 121a.5[9]).

Learning-disabled children can learn effectively if they are provided the types of experiences that enable them to acquire and retain information more efficiently and permit them to enhance their self-esteem. But if a learning-disabled child is not provided the type of supportive experiences he requires during his early years (birth to eight or nine years of age), the learning disability will usually have a negative effect on the child's self-esteem, which in turn impedes the child's ability to develop his or her potential effectively.

Parent strategies. The following strategies are recommended for parents in helping their children with reading, spelling, and arithmetic.

Reading.

1. Parents should expose their children to reading tasks that are short and fairly simple initially, and increase the complexity of the tasks gradually to ensure success and minimize failure.
2. Parents should cooperate closely with teachers, and coordinate the tasks they provide for their child with those being offered at school.
3. Parents should use a structured approach when teaching their children to read—an approach that uses both visual and auditory modalities.

Spelling.

1. Parents should expose their children to spelling words that are fairly simple (e.g., one-syllable) initially, and increase the length and complexity of the words gradually.
2. Parents should ensure that spelling assignments that are not completed at school be completed at home. The child should work independently, however, and be provided assistance only when it is apparent that assistance is needed.
3. The Fitzgerald Method is a technique that parents can use to teach their children spelling. When using the Fitzgerald Method, the recommended sequence is:
   a. Have the child look at the word.
   b. Have the child pronounce the word.
   c. Have the child pronounce the word again with eyes closed.
   d. Cover up the word and have the child write it.
   e. If the word is spelled incorrectly, begin the se-

quence again.
4. Parents should also use a neurolinguistic approach to teach spelling. When using a neurolinguistic approach, the recommended sequence is:
   a. Write the word the child is to spell on a card.
   b. Show the card to the child.
   c. Remove the card from the child's view.
   d. Teach the child to use visual imagery or construct pictures of the word to be spelled.
   e. Have the child spell the word forward.
   f. Then, have the child spell the word backwards.

Arithmetic.

1. Parents should expose their children to simple arithmetic tasks initially, and increase the complexity of the tasks gradually.
2. Parents should teach the child how to use internal dialogue, in which he repeats the task or question to himself and then generates the appropriate image or picture which permits him to answer the question.
3. Parents should use visual imagery to teach multiplication facts. Once the facts have been learned, they should be stored for future use. Flashcards are helpful.
4. Parents should use money to teach arithmetic concepts to their children.
5. Parents should use unusual materials to arouse their children's curiosity regarding basic quantitative concepts. For example, use world records, athletic statistics, weights, and heights.
6. Parents should use games to teach arithmetic concepts. Examples are Old Maid, Chutes and Ladders, Dominoes, and Picture Lotto.

Teacher strategies. Teachers should function as advocates of all children, and this disposition should be especially strong for the learning-disabled child. Thus, the teacher should provide much encouragement and support. The following strategies are recommended for teachers to use with learning-disabled students in reading, spelling, and arithmetic.

Reading.

1. Teachers should provide the child reading tasks that are short and fairly simple initially, and increase the complexity of the tasks gradually.
2. Teachers should use a systematic, structured approach to reading that emphasizes both visual and auditory modalities.
3. Teachers should use a revisualization process to teach sight words. The recommended sequence is:
   a. Have the child look at a flashcard with a new sight word printed on it, and have the child repeat the word after it is pronounced to him.
   b. Have the child trace the word in the air, using his entire, extended arm, pointing and tracing with the pointer and index fingers. If the child forms any of the letters of the word incorrectly, have him repeat the process while spelling the word orally.
   c. Have the child close his eyes and try to revisualize the sequence of letters that make the word. Then, tell him to trace the word from memory, spelling it aloud simultaneously with his eyes closed, trying to see a picture of the letters while he is performing this task.
   d. Have the child test himself by writing the word from memory. If he cannot write the word from memory, show him the word again, and repeat the earlier steps a, b, and c. Remind the child to spell the word subvocally ("under his breath") as he writes, and to repeat the word before he writes it and again after he writes it.
   e. Give the child a group of flashcards that include the word being taught and other words of a similar configuration—for example: friend, frend, freind, frand . . . .
4. Teachers should encourage the child to read to the class, starting with easy material and gradually increasing its complexity.

Spelling.

1. Teachers should provide spelling words and lists

that are short and fairly simple initially, and gradually increase the length and complexity.
2. Teachers should use the Fitzgerald Method to teach spelling. This is the same as was described for parents.
3. Teachers should use a neurolinguistic approach to teach spelling—again, the same as described for parents.
4. Teachers should use a "communicative competence" approach to teach children to spell. The teacher employing this approach will:
   a. Incorporate the words to be spelled into an oral discussion to enable students to understand how they are pronounced and used in a meaningful context.
   b. Have students identify the words to be spelled visually on the chalkboard. Then, give pupils worksheets comprised of groups of four or five words that are similar in configuration—for example: friend, frond, frend, freind, frand . . . .
   c. Have students identify the word that is spelled correctly and write it for review.
   d. Have students use the word correctly in both oral and written sentences.
5. Teachers can use a star chart or similar reward system to recognize improved performance.

Arithmetic.

1. Teachers should provide students simple arithmetic tasks at first, and gradually increase complexity.
2. Teachers should teach how to use internal dialogue (as described in parent strategies) to solve arithmetic tasks.
3. Teachers should use a visual imagery sequence to teach multiplication facts (the same as parent strategies).
4. Teachers should present arithmetic tasks in a sequence which permits the child to perform all of the complementary operations and at the same time learn basic facts. The recommended sequence is illustrated by the following:

$$\begin{array}{ll} 9 & 3 \\ \underline{\times 3} & \underline{\times 9} \\ 27 & 27 \end{array} \qquad 3\overline{)27} \quad 9\overline{)27} \qquad 3\times 9 = 27 \quad 9\times 3 = 27$$

5. Teachers may use long but simple problems to help students "overlearn" operations and facts.

$$\begin{array}{rrr} 888 & 321{,}742{,}134{,}521 & 892{,}678{,}542 \\ \underline{-333} & \underline{+134{,}151{,}341{,}237} & \underline{-151{,}265{,}321} \end{array}$$

Although data derived from the literature indicate that approximately 10 to 15 percent of children experience learning disabilities, parents and teachers need to realize that some pupils manifest inauthentic or pseudo-learning disabilities (Battle 1985); and it is important to be able to differentiate between the two. As I have stated elsewhere (1985), *authentic* learning disabilities are tied to a neurological base in which some form of dysfunction impedes the student's ability to process certain types of stimuli associated with learning; whereas *inauthentic* or pseudo-learning disabilities are due to psychological rather than neurological factors. The following report of Trudy is presented here to illustrate a case of pseudo-learning disability.

Case Report 6:1. Trudy; 20 years, 5 months.
Low self-esteem, depression, and pseudo-learning disability.

Trudy was the only girl and oldest child in a family with two children. Her mother reported that the pregnancy was normal but a Caesarian section had to be performed during birth. The attending physician stated that he felt Trudy would be mentally retarded. Trudy was a hyperactive and unaffectionate child during the first six months of her life. She subsequently became more affectionate, but continued to be very active. With the exception of the "hyperactivity," Trudy's early developent was generally normal. She crawled at 8 months, walked at 12 months, and was toilet trained at 24 months. Trudy started to use sentences at 18 months, and could identify words at two and a half years.

Trudy experienced considerable behavioral difficulties in first and second grade because of her "hyperactivity." When she was in second grade, her doctor prescribed methylphenidate (Ritalin) for her hyperactivity, but her mother took her off this medication after a year because "it didn't work." Trudy was subsequently prescribed sleeping pills, but took them only for a short period of time because they, too, "didn't work."

Trudy's mother reported that Trudy was always a good reader but that she was poorly coordinated, had difficulties writing, and generally produced "messy" work. Trudy's mother said that she performed very well in arithmetic until the fourth grade; but, once the problem began, it continued throughout the rest of her school career. As a result of her academic problems, Trudy did not complete the requirements for high school graduation. Rather than re-enroll in the public school system, she transferred to a private parochial school to complete the remaining requirements for graduation. She experienced academic and emotional difficulties in this new setting, however, and attempted suicide by taking an overdose of sleeping pills. Shortly thereafter, Trudy's parents joined a support group for parents of children with learning disabilities. Trudy's parents stated that the insights and information they received while attending sessions sponsored by this group were beneficial, but Trudy continued to experience academic problems.

In a "final" effort, Trudy's parents referred her to a psychologist for psychotherapy. Her WAIS Verbal, Performance, and Full Scale IQ scores were 122, 102, and 114 respectively. Trudy's neurological system was intact, and she was not experiencing any form of learning disability. Personality tests indicated that her self-esteem was very low and that she was depressed. Analysis of self-esteem and arithmetic scores are presented here:

. . . .

Score

	Possible	Mean	Actual	%-ile	t	Class.
Total	32	23.7	13	6	33	v. low
General	16	12.0	5	5	32	low
Social	8	6.9	5	22	43	inter.
Personal	8	4.4	3	39	47	low

Arithmetic Computation

Timed Graded Score	4.7
Untimed Graded Score	6.6

. . . .

Trudy was provided psychotherapy to assist her in resolving her psychosocial problems; she received individual tutoring in arithmetic to help her acquire greater computational skills. After eight weeks of treatment, Trudy was reassessed. At this time she was not depressed, and her self-esteem and arithmetic computation scores had improved. The results of the reassessment follow:

. . . .

Score

	Possible	Mean	Actual	%-ile	t	Class.
Total	32	23.7	24	54	53	inter.
General	16	12.0	11	44	50	inter.
Social	8	6.9	5	22	43	inter.
Personal	8	4.9	8	95	65	v. high

Arithmetic Computation

Timed Graded Score	10.5
Untimed Graded Score	11.0

. . . .

The Gifted Child

A gifted child is one who scores 135 or better on the *Wechsler Intelligence Scale for Children, Revised* or 140 or better on the *Stanford-Binet Intelligence Test.* Performance on standardized intelligence tests, however, is not the only variable determining "giftedness." For instance, Witty (1952) defined gifted children as those "whose performance is consistently remarkable in music, art, social leadership, and other forms of expression." Witty's definition, which was adopted by the American Association for Gifted Children, is a broad one that does not limit the gifted to those who score above a certain point on a standardized intelligence test, but includes those with creative talent in an almost unlimited range of socially useful endeavors. The gifted are generally creative, innovative children who are typically above average in academic achievement.

Parent strategies.

1. Parents of the gifted should provide their children with a diversity of experiences intended to promote creative curiosity and novel methods of inquiry.
2. Parents should provide their gifted children with experiences that promote the development of imagination and creative resourcefulness.
3. Parents of the gifted should promote the development of reasonable aspirations in their children, rather than those that are too high or too low.

Teacher strategies.

1. Teachers of the gifted should provide them with tasks that challenge their ability, creativity, and resourcefulness.
2. Teachers of the gifted should encourage them to use their potential to the fullest and permit them to undertake self-selected projects after they have completed regularly assigned tasks.
3. Teachers of the gifted should assist these children in developing and expanding their exceptional potential by encouraging them to share their insights with others.
4. Teachers should encourage their gifted children to

conduct independent studies and report their findings to classmates and other interested groups.
5. Teachers should provide their gifted children with tasks that require complex associative methods rather than simple, direct, rote drill.
6. Teachers should provide their gifted students with experiences that enable them to engage in creative inquiry.
7. Teachers should provide their gifted pupils opportunities to apply principles and theories to real-life situations.

The Emotionally Disordered Child

If a child is experiencing significant emotional problems, he or she should be referred to a qualified therapist, and parents and teachers should work cooperatively with the therapist. The role of the therapist is to differentially diagnose the child's condition, provide the child some insights into the problems at hand, assist in clarifying the problems more precisely, and teach the child to resolve the problems by exploring alternatives, assessing the probable consequences of each option, and choosing modes of behaving that are self-enhancing, rather than self-defeating.

Although the therapist will work with the child for a period of time (usually, one hour per week), the child will continue to spend most of the time in his or her regular social milieu. Parents and teachers, therefore, should develop strategies or competencies which they can use to assist the child in developing more effective psychosocial skills. These skills, in turn, enable the child to adjust more appropriately and develop personal potential more effectively.

The emotionally disordered child is one who is experiencing clinically significant difficulties in adjusting to the ordinary cultural demands placed upon individuals within his or her age group. Some strategies that parents and teachers can employ are:

Parent strategies.

1. Parents of the overly anxious child should:

a. Communicate to the child that he or she is worthy, significant, and accepted.
b. Communicate to the child that he or she is loved unconditionally—"You don't have to be perfect to be loved and accepted."
c. Permit the child to express feelings openly, without fear of reprimand or rejection.
2. Parents of a child who feels inferior should:
a. Emphasize positive aspects of the child's behavior, rather than negative ones.
b. Provide the child with encouragement and assist him in developing greater self-confidence.
c. Provide the child firm, consistent support.
d. Involve the child in activities at home that foster closer parent-child relationships.
3. Parents of the school-phobic child should:
a. Establish reinforcement schedules at home and reward the child for regular school attendance.
b. Establish a structured schedule which is adhered-to consistently when the child is absent from school. The child should be required to sit at a table and do the work assigned by the teacher, via the mother or father. The child should receive only the breaks (e.g., recess) at home that he or she does regularly at school. No television or other forms of diversion should be permitted until work assignments are completed and the regular school time is . over.

Teacher strategies.

1. When interacting with overly anxious children, teachers should:
a. Encourage the child to relax during tests and permit him or her to take tests orally if there is a tendency to "freeze up" when writing exams.
b. Encourage parents to lower their standards if the child's anxieties are due to unrealistic parental expectations.
c. Not expose the anxious student to any form of ridicule or sarcasm.

2. Teachers of children who feel inferior should:
    a. Emphasize strengths rather than weaknesses, and create learning experiences to ensure success.
    b. Assign the child esteemed roles (e.g., tutoring other students, serving on committees).
    c. Assist the child in becoming more assertive, and encourage him or her to participate in class discussions.
    d. Provide the student short assignments that can be easily finished, and offer rewards for that completion.
    e. Ensure that the child is exposed to a consistent model of behavior in school. If the child has more than one teacher, all should meet and decide among themselves how the child is to be treated.
3. Teachers of school-phobic children should:
    a. Establish reinforcement schedules at school to reward the child for regular attendance.
    b. Communicate regularly with parents, initially on a daily basis, with fewer contacts as improvement in attendance occurs.

The Behaviorally Disordered Child

The behaviorally disordered child, like his or her emotionally disordered counterpart, should be referred to a certified psychotherapist, and parents and teachers should work in concert with the therapist. The services that the psychotherapist provides for the child displaying behavior problems are similar to those provided for children experiencing emotional problems, in terms of diagnosing condition, providing insights, helping in clarification of problems, and assisting in the modification of self-defeating patterns.

The behaviorally disordered child is one who consistently displays behavior that is significantly deviant from the social "norm" for individuals of the same age and cultural setting. Here are some strategies that parents and teachers can use:

Parent strategies.

1. Parents of the behaviorally disordered child should:
   a. Provide clearly defined limits that are enforced consistently.
   b. Encourage the child to manage behavior more "appropriately," and require him to deal with the consequences of his actions.
   c. Facilitate the development of "appropriate" behavior by offering rewards (e.g., permission to participate in preferred self-selected activities, giving attention) when behavior meets expectations.
   d. Emphasize positive aspects of the child's behavior, not negative ones.
   e. Expose the child to reinforcement contingencies designed to promote desirable behavior and extinguish undesirable behavior.

Teacher strategies.

1. Teachers of the behaviorally disordered child should:
   a. Provide the child with a structured classroom environment with clearly defined limits that are enforced consistently.
   b. Clarify expectations for the child and require him to deal with the consequences of his actions.
   c. Emphasize positive rather than negative aspects of the child's behavior and reprimand only when absolutely necessary. In those few instances, reprimand as privately and quietly as possible.
   d. Permit the child to work in an environment that has little stimulation (e.g., a cubicle) when behavior is disruptive enough to impede the progress of other students.
   e. Allow the child to take "time out" or remove himself from the classroom when he becomes frustrated or when behavior is disruptive.
   f. Expose the child to reinforcement contingencies designed to promote desirable behavior and extinguish undesirable behavior.

g. Provide the child support, encourage him to manage his behavior more effectively, and permit him to deal with the consequences of his actions.

h. Offer legitimate rewards for appropriate behavior.

i. Provide a highly structured, comprehensive program that attends to both cognitive (academic) and affective (emotional, behavioral) needs.

The Troubled, Unemployed Youth

The predicament of the troubled, unemployed youth deserves special mention. The individual who has less-than-average self-esteem, coupled with a relatively low level of education, and no job, is at high risk for a lifetime of problems for the person himself and for his society. The following describes results of a program that seems to have merit for those young adults who have already begun to develop self-defeating patterns of behavior.

In 1986 our research group conducted a study designed to determine the effects that a comprehensive job training strategy have on the self-esteem of participating trainees. An additional purpose of the study was to determine the effects that psychotherapy have on the self-esteem of trainees.

Forty males and females enrolled in a job training program agreed to participate, but, although 40 subjects were assessed initially, the number was reduced to 22 because 7 (17.5 percent) left the program early to take jobs; 6 (15 percent) were terminated because they refused to comply with the rules and regulations; and 5 (12 percent) simply dropped out, so their status is unknown. Fifteen (68 percent) of the 22 who completed the program obtained employment when the program ended; of the total group of 40, 22 (55 percent) altogether found jobs.

All subjects participating in the study were unemployed prior to enrollment; and most had been without work for six months or more. The mean age for participating subjects was 21 years, 8 months; the mean level of formal education was 10 years, 3 months.

A significant number of those who participated in the study experienced a wide variety of adjustment difficulties over the years—including learning disabilities, school failure, emotional and behavioral problems, alcohol and drug abuse, alienation, and delinquency. Of these participants, 55 percent had experienced difficulties with the legal system that were severe enough to result in charges being laid against them. Forty-five percent of the subjects had spent at least one night in jail, and the length of incarceration ranged from one day to four years.

In addition to the regular training program, which incorporated classroom instruction and on-site job training in auto mechanics, trainees were provided the opportunity to participate, on a voluntary basis, in a number of enhancement activities (e.g., driver training, academic upgrading) and receive psychotherapy.

The self-esteem scores of the group. All of those participating in the study were administered the *Culture-Free Self-Esteem Inventory for Adults*, the first occurring during November, 1985. Posttesting was conducted during January, 1986. Follow-up was in June, 1986. All subjects read the items independently, and French and Spanish versions were provided for those who requested them. The inventory was administered to the group by the author, but those who were absent during group testing completed the inventory independently in the presence of the project coordinator.

Findings of the study for the total group are presented in table 6:1. Table 6:1 presents means, standard deviations, and the significance associated with the means earned by the participants on three occasions.

Data displayed in Table 6:1 indicate that the group experienced significant positive shifts in total self-esteem and in all facets. It is also worthwhile to note that, meanwhile, the lie scores of participants (which indicate defensiveness, lack of trust, or unwillingness to reveal things about oneself) did not vary significantly, indicating that subjects consistently provided authentic responses regarding their perceptions of self-worth.

Table 6:2 presents the means, standard deviations, and significance associated with the means earned by those group members who received psychotherapy.

TABLE 6:1. *Means, Standard Deviations, and Significance for All Training Program Subjects (N = 40).*

	Pretest Mean	S.D.	Posttest Mean	S.D.	Follow-Up Mean	S.D.	p
Total	20.70	6.46	22.70	4.56	26.05	3.61	.01
General	10.11	3.87	10.76	2.51	12.70	2.36	.01
Social	5.58	1.41	6.35	1.22	7.29	0.92	.01
Personal	5.00	2.71	5.47	2.03	6.05	1.71	.05
Lie	4.94	1.81	5.52	1.94	6.05	1.43	.30

TABLE 6:2. *Means, Standard Deviations, and Significance for Training Program Subjects in Therapy (N = 7).*

	Pretest Mean	S.D.	Posttest Mean	S.D.	Follow-Up Mean	S.D.	p
Total	21.75	6.99	26.00	4.24	29.00	2.44	.01
General	11.00	4.08	14.00	2.00	13.75	1.50	.01
Social	5.50	2.08	6.75	0.95	7.75	0.50	.01
Personal	5.25	3.20	5.25	2.75	7.70	1.00	.01
Lie	5.00	2.16	5.50	2.38	5.50	2.38	.81

Analysis of variance of scores earned by subjects who received psychotherapy during the pre- and posttesting indicate that they experienced significant positive shifts in total self-esteem and in all facets. It is worthwhile to note that the gains in self-esteem scores by those who received psychotherapy are greater than gains for those who did not.

Discussion. Findings of the study confirm previous data which suggest that unemployment has a negative effect on one's self-esteem. For instance, the total mean self-esteem score for trainees was significantly lower (20.70) than that of the standardization group (23.7) when the program commenced; but it was higher than that of the standardization group when the program terminated (26.05). Gains in self-esteem scores were even higher for trainees who received psychotherapy: from 21.75 to 29.0.

That trainees who received psychotherapy experienced greater gains in all facets of self-esteem than those who did not, provides support for researchers and clinicians who propose that self-esteem is an important variable which is associated with psychopathology (e.g., Branden 1969) and mental health (e.g., Coopersmith 1967).

Findings of the study indicate that, as the mean scores for subjects increased, their standard deviations decreased— resulting in greater homogeneity of scores. This trend was particularly strong for trainees who received psychotherapy. These data indicate that treatment exerted a strong positive effect on the self-esteem of participants, and that subjects who earned lower self-esteem scores initially experienced greater gains in self-esteem than did those who earned higher scores initially.

Prospects for the future. Although this study demonstrates quite clearly that positive shifts in the self-esteem of unemployed young adults can be induced by exposing them to a comprehensive job training strategy, there is a need to conduct further research using control subjects in which follow-up is provided to determine the long-term effects that training programs such as this one have on the self-esteem of participants. An important application of these findings is that the self-esteem of unemployed youth experiencing adjustment problems can be significantly enhanced—if they are provided effective intervention. These data strongly indicate that there is an important need to develop and implement programs such as the one described in this chapter much more widely than is the case at present.

The following two case reports are presented to illustrate the effects that this comprehensive job training program had on selected trainees who received psychotherapy.

Case Report 6:2. Trisha; 20 years, 5 months.
Anxiety disorder with depression.

Trisha was the second youngest child in a family in which there were two boys and three girls. Trisha was a twin, but her sister died at birth. Trisha's mother reported that her pregnancy and development during the early years were normal. Trisha walked at 1 year, started to use sentences at 20 months, and was toilet trained when she reached 2 years. Trisha experienced Cushing's Syndrome when she was 10 years old, and had to take daily treatments for this disorder for 10 months. Trisha's physician also prescribed medication to accelerate her growth, which he felt was "stunted" as a side-effect of the treatment she received for Cushing's Syndrome. This intervention, however, was not successful; Trisha is the shortest person in her family and is significantly shorter than the typical person her age.

Trisha enrolled in kindergarten at age 4 years, 6 months, and generally earned good grades in elementary, junior high, and high school. As a result of her weight problem, however, the children in elementary school teased her, frequently calling her names such as "Fatso." The teasing was not as frequent in junior and senior high school, but she continued to have difficulties in her interpersonal relationships with peers.

Trisha graduated from high school at the age of 18, but was unable to obtain steady employment. Thus, at the age of 19 she entered a publicly sponsored worker's entry training program and shortly afterwards was referred to the program's consulting psychologist because of her "low self-esteem and limited ability to establish positive relationships with peers." In his diagnosis, the psychologist indicated that Trisha had an anxiety disorder with associated depression. Trisha's WAIS Verbal, Performance, and Full Scale IQ scores were 99, 116, and 106 respectively. An analysis of her self-esteem scores revealed the following:

. . . .

			Score			
	Possible	Mean	Actual	%-ile	t	Class.
Total	32	24.1	23	47	51	inter.
General	16	12.0	15	93	63	v. high
Social	8	6.9	6	44	51	high
Personal	8	4.9	2	25	43	low

. . . .

After eight months, Trisha quit the automotive training program she was placed in because she "didn't enjoy this type of work," and obtained a position as a secretary. She adjusted so well in this environment that the employer encouraged her to apply for a permanent position. Trisha, however, chose to enroll in a teacher's aide training program at a local community college.

After 17 weeks of psychotherapy, Trisha was able to resolve her emotional problems, was generally adjusting satisfactorily, and was able to establish relationships with peers that were positive and mutually beneficial. At this time, an analysis of her self-esteem scores revealed the following:

. . . .

		Score				
	Possible	Mean	Actual	%-ile	t	Class.
Total	32	24.1	31	98	66	v. high
General	16	12.0	15	93	63	v. high
Social	8	6.9	8	78	59	v. high
Personal	8	4.9	8	95	65	v. high

. . . .

Case Report 6:3. Tom; 21 years, 3 months.
Hypomania and impulsivity.

Tom's development during the early years was generally normal. The birth process was normal. He walked at 10 months, started to use sentences at 18 months, and was toilet trained at 2 years, 4 months.

Tom enrolled in kindergarten at 4 years, 6 months; and his adjustment during the elementary and junior high school years was generally satisfactory. During this period he was a highly motivated student who earned excellent grades; but his achievement pattern changed dramatically in his third year of high school, when his parents separated. Prior to his parents' separation, Tom was a highly creative, artistic student who was an active individual, but somewhat of a loner;

and on two occasions, he had been caught stealing inexpensive items that he collected. When his parents separated, Tom's behavior became profoundly "deviant"; and he was expelled from school.

After expulsion, Tom attempted suicide and was seen by a psychiatrist on one occasion. Shortly thereafter, he joined a publicly sponsored job entry training program. He continued to have adjustment difficulties and conduct problems which resulted in legal prosecution and the possibility of incarceration. At this time, Tom asked to see the program's consulting psychologist because he was awaiting trial by judge for his "kleptomania" problem—a behavior that manifested itself beginning when Tom was 10 years old.

When psychotherapy commenced, Tom's self-esteem was within the Intermediate level, and he was not depressed; but he was a moderately hypomanic individual with weak impulse control. He was experiencing confusion in thinking and determining what was "appropriate" and "inappropriate." His WAIS Verbal, Performance, and Full Scale IQ scores were 117, 128, and 123 respectively. Analysis of Tom's self-esteem scores revealed the following:

		Score			
	Possible	Mean	Actual	%-ile	t	Class.
Total	32	24.1	21	34	46	inter.
General	16	12.0	7	7	34	low
Social	8	6.9	6	51	52	high
Personal	8	4.9	8	90	63	v. high

Tom experienced considerable difficulties during the initial stages of psychotherapy that impeded progress somewhat. For instance, while drinking with friends, he accompanied them in stealing some small object of little value—which resulted in charges being laid against him (making his third brush with the authorities). Also, he changed residences on four occasions; and his father's common-law wife committed suicide. He was able to endure all of these traumas, however, and make steady progress in spite of them. After 11 weeks of therapy, Tom quit his automotive training program and was able to obtain a training position in an "artistic" field which was more appropriate for his ability, aptitude, and interest. After 25 weeks of therapy, Tom was able to resolve his major difficulties and modify his self-defeating patterns. Testing at this time indicated that he was adjusting quite satisfactorily. Analysis of his self-esteem scores revealed the following:

. . . .

Score

	Possible	Mean	Actual	%-ile	t	Class.
Total	32	24.1	27	75	58	high
General	16	12.0	13	71	57	high
Social	8	6.9	7	80	60	high
Personal	8	4.9	7	73	57	high

. . . .

SUMMARY

1. Exceptional children require specialized forms of aid in order to develop their potential fully.
2. Experts disagree in their assumptions regarding what a "learning disability" is. Definitions of what a learning disability is tend to vary.
3. Learning-disabled students can learn effectively if they are provided the types of experiences that enable them to acquire and retain information more efficiently, and permit them to enhance their self-esteem.
4. The learning disabled, gifted, emotionally disordered, behaviorally disordered, and the unemployed

youth, are exceptional groups who require specialized forms of facilitation.

IV

RECOMMENDED READINGS AND REFERENCES

RECOMMENDED READINGS

Books and Papers

Anderson, K. 1979. The effects of the Magic Circle program on the self-concepts of children in grades four and five. Master's thesis. Edmonton, Alberta: University of Alberta.

>In this study, conducted as part of a master's thesis, the author investigates the effects that the Magic Circle program have on the self-concepts of participating students.

Battle, J. 1972. The effects of a tutoring program on the self-esteem and academic achievement of elementary students. Doctoral dissertation. Edmonton, Alberta: University of Alberta.

>The author reports that fifth- and sixth-grade students who functioned as tutors of younger children experienced significant gains in spelling achievement.

Battle, J. 1982. *Enhancing self-esteem and achievement.* Seattle: Special Child Publications.

>The text provides a comprehensive overview of the phenomena that constitute self-esteem. How self-esteem and achievement interact and complement

each other is clearly delineated, and the author provides empirically tested strategies and techniques that enhance self-esteem and achievement. Twenty-six inventories that assess perception of self-worth are described.

Branden, N. 1969. *The psychology of self-esteem.* Los Angeles: Nash Publishing.

The author presents the point of view which holds that self-esteem is a fundamental human need, and that various levels of self-esteem are consequences of our use of the freedom to think or not to think.

Branden, N. 1980. *Breaking free.* Los Angeles: Tharcher.

The author offers 22 case reports that deal with the childhood origins of negative perceptions of self-worth.

Branden, N. 1980. *The disowned self.* Los Angeles: Tharcher.

Provides an overview of the problem of self-alienation.

Briggs, D. C. 1970. *Your child's self-esteem.* Garden City, New York: Doubleday.

This book gives an overview of self-esteem and offers suggestions for parents to promote self-esteem.

Brookover, W. B., and Thomas, S. 1964. *A sociology of education*, 2nd ed. New York: American Book Company.

The authors provide data indicating a significant relationship between self-concept and achievement.

Burns, R. B. 1979. *The self-concept in theory, measurement, development, and behavior.* London: Longman.

The author proposes that the self-concept is the composite image of what we think we are, what we think we can achieve, what we think others think of us, and what we would like to do.

Coopersmith, S. 1967. *Antecedents of self-esteem.* San Francisco: W. H. Freeman.

The author examines antecedents that contribute to the development of high self-esteem.

Cummings, R. N. 1971. A study of the relationship between self-concepts and reading achievement at the third-grade level. Doctoral dissertation. University of Alabama. Microfilm. Ann Arbor, Michigan: University Microfilms.

Findings of the study indicate that self-concept is significantly related to reading achievement.

Dinkmeyer, D., and Dreikurs, R. 1963. *Encouraging children to learn: the encouragement process.* Englewood Cliffs, New Jersey: Prentice-Hall.

Solutions to problem-solving, in this text, emphasize encouragement in the learning process and deemphasize conflict and confrontation.

Hamachek, D. E. 1971. *Encounters with the self.* New York: Holt, Rinehart, and Winston.

Here, awareness of self begins at birth; self-perception is determined, in part, by how we perceive ourselves as really being, how we ideally perceive ourselves, and how we feel others perceive us.

Hamachek, D. E. 1978. *Encounters with the self.* New York: Holt, Rinehart, and Winston.

The author discusses the various components of the self and describes how a healthy self-concept develops.

Jersild, A. T. 1952. *In search of self.* New York: Teachers College Press.

According to the authors, schools should take an active role in promoting self-understanding.

Labenne, W. D., and Green, B. I. 1969. *Educational implications of self-concept theory.* Pacific Palisades, California: Goodyear Publishing.

Gives an overview of self-concept theory and offers views regarding how information derived from self-concept theory can promote educational advances.

Murphy, G. 1975. *Outgrowing self-deception.* New York: Basic Books.

The author examines the human need to perceive the self as worthy, and how people may strive to protect themselves from negative self-feeling through self-deception.

Peterson, K. M. 1980. An investigation of self-esteem and related variables of educationally mentally handicapped students. Master's thesis. Edmonton, Alberta: University of Alberta.

The study reports findings which indicate that the self-esteem of mentally retarded students is significantly related to teachers' ratings of their behavior.

Purkey, W. W. 1970. *Self-concept and school achievement.* Englewood Cliffs, New Jersey: Prentice-Hall.

The book gives an historical review of the various theories that deal with the self, and lists characteristics of the self.

Raimy, V. 1975. *Misunderstandings of the self.* San Francisco: Jossey-Bass.

The author offers a "misconception" hypothesis, in which he indicates that people can resolve emotional problems by eliminating faulty ideas and beliefs.

Rosenberg, M. 1979. *Conceiving the self.* New York: Basic Books.

dividual's frame of reference, or the foundation on which actions are predicated, and proposes that self-esteem and self-consistency are distinct motives which guide human behavior.

Samuels, S. C. 1977. *Enhancing self-concept in early childhood: theory and practice.* New York: Human Sciences.

This book proposes that early childhood is the most critical period for the development of self-concept, and that a key goal of parents and teachers of children under the age of six should be to enhance their perceptions of self-worth.

Simon, N. 1976. *Why am I different?* New York: A. Whitman.

realistic self-image is essential for positive psychological growth.

Snygg, D., and Combs, A. W. 1959. *Individual behavior.* New York: Harper and Row.

The fundamental thesis of this book is that the perceptual field of each human being determines his or her behavior in every instance.

Thomas, J. B. 1973. *Self-concept in psychology and education: a review of research.* New York: Humanities Press.

The book presents the position that the self is a learned structure that is more influenced by interactions with parents and other family members than it is by social class.

Wylie, R. 1961. *The self-concept: a critical survey of pertinent research literature.* Lincoln, Nebraska: University of Nebraska Press.

A review of research conducted prior to 1961.

Yaniw, L. 1983. The relationship between three affective variables and student achievement. Master's thesis. Edmonton, Alberta: University of Alberta.

The study reports findings which confirm that achievement is related to self-esteem, and that this relationship appears to be fairly independent of measured intelligence.

Articles, Presentations, and Reports

Battle, J. 1978. Relationship between self-esteem and depression. *Psychological Reports* 42:745-746.

Findings confirm the relationship between self-esteem and depression in adults is significant; as depression intensifies, self-esteem diminishes.

Battle, J. 1980. Relationship between self-esteem and depression among high school students. *Perceptual and Motor Skills* 51.157-158.

Findings confirm the relationship between self-esteem and depression in adolescents is significant.

Battle, J. 1981. Enhancing self-esteem: a new challenge to teachers. *Academic Therapy* (May) 16:5, pp. 541-550.

The article delineates the important role that self-esteem plays in the educative process, and encourages teachers to accept the challenge of addressing both cognitive and affective needs of pupils.

Battle, J. 1984. Relationship between self-esteem and depression among children. Edmonton, Alberta: Edmonton Public Schools.

The data reported indicate that the relationship between self-esteem and depression in children is similar to that of adolescents and adults.

Battle, J. 1983. The teacher's role in the enhancement of self-esteem and achievement. *Prime Areas* (Winter) 25:2.

Teachers can exert a strong effect on their students' self-esteem; the author encourages teachers to interact positively with students.

Battle, J., and Blowers, T. G. 1982. A longitudinal comparative study of the self-esteem of students in regular and special classes. *Journal of Learning Disabilities* (February) 15:2.

Self-esteem of learning-disabled and regular students is compared; effects that special class placement have on learning-disabled students over a three-year period are described.

Battle, J., and Yanish, D. L. 1985. Relationship between self-esteem, depression, and alcohol consumption among adolescents. *Psychological Reports* 57:331-334.

Findings cited here confirm previous observations that indicate that self-esteem and depression are significantly related; alcohol consumption is associated with the various facets of self-esteem as measured by the *Culture-Free Self-Esteem Inventory for Children.*

Beane, J. 1973. Self-concept and self-esteem as curriculum issues. *Today's Education (NEA Journal).*

The author proposes that one's concept of ability influences achievement; achievement, in turn, influences one's concept of ability.

Campbell, L. 1981. Improving self-image. North Texas State University *NASSD Bulletin* (Denton).

The authors argue that negative self-concept is the most crucial variable impeding academic achievement in students, preventing them from developing their potential fully.

Charalampous, K. D., Ford, K. F., and Skinner, T. J. 1976. Self-esteem in alcoholics and nonalcoholics. *Journal of Studies on Alcohol* 37:990-994.

Findings indicate that alcoholism is associated with level of self-esteem.

Fahey, M., and Phillips, S. 1981. The self-concept in middle childhood: some baseline data. *Child Study Journal* 11:3, pp. 155-165.

The thesis here holds that self-concept grows or develops during middle childhood.

Kidwell, J. 1982. The neglected birth order: middleborns. *Journal of Marriage and the Family* pp. 225-235.

Reported findings indicate that middleborn children possess lower levels of self-esteem than first- or last-born children.

Mitic, W. R. 1980. Alcohol use and self-esteem of adolescents. *Journal of Drug Education* 10:197-208.

Data reported indicate that individuals who drink alcohol on a regular basis possess significantly lower levels of self-esteem than those who do not drink.

Staines, J. W. 1958. The development of children's values: the self-picture as a factor in the classroom. *British Journal of Educational Psychology* 18:97-111.

The article delineates the important effects that self-esteem have in behavior and achievement. The author says that the self is the major component of the personality, and encourages teachers to make concerted efforts to improve the self-perceptions of their pupils.

Stevenson, D. T., and Romney, D. M. 1984. Depression in learning-disabled children. *Journal of Learning Disabilities* 10:579-582.

The article gives data supporting the position that self-esteem is significantly associated with depression in children.

Watson, J. 1973. How to change negative self-concepts in low-ability children. *Today's Education (NEA Journal)* pp. 26-27.

Strategies are offered for teachers to use in improving the self-concepts of children with low ability.

Wattenberg, M. W., and Clifford, C. 1964. Relationship of self-concepts to beginning achievement in reading. *Child Development* 35:461-467.

The study indicates that positive self-concept is an antecedent of reading, and that self-concept scores can be used to predict subsequent reading achievement.

REFERENCES

Adler, A. 1927. *The practice and therapy of individual psychology.* New York: Harcourt.

Allen, U. L., and Feldman, R. S. 1972. Learning through tutoring: low achieving children as tutors. Technical report no. 236. Madison, Wisconsin: University of Wisconsin.

Allport, G. W. 1961. *Pattern and growth in personality.* New York: Holt, Rinehart, and Winston.

American Psychiatric Association. 1980. *Diagnostic and statistical manual of mental disorders.* Washington, D.C.

Aronson, E.; Blaney, N.; Sikes, J.; Stephan, C.; and Snapp, M. 1975. Busing and racial tension: the jigsaw route to learning and liking. *Psychology Today* (February) pp. 43-50.

Battle, J.
1975. Comparative study of the self-esteem of deviant and nondeviant students. Edmonton, Alberta: Edmonton Public Schools.

1977. Test-retest reliability of the Canadian [culture-free] self-esteem inventory for children. Edmonton, Alberta: Edmonton Public Schools.

1978. Relationship between self-esteem and depression. *Psychological Reports* 42:745-746.

1979. Self-esteem of students in regular and special classes. *Psychological Reports* 42:212-214.

1980. Relationship between self-esteem and depression among high school students. *Perceptual and Motor Skills* 51:157-158.

1981a. *Culture-free self-esteem inventories for children and adults.* Seattle: Special Child Publications.

1981b. Enhancing self-esteem: a new challenge to teachers. *Academic Therapy* (May) 16:5, pp. 541-550.

1982. *Enhancing self-esteem and achievement.* Seattle: Special Child Publications.

1983. The teacher's role in the enhancement of self-esteem and achievement. *Prime Areas* (Winter) 25:2.

1985. *Effective parenting tips that build self-esteem.* Seattle: Special Child Publications.

19—. *Psychopathology: a practical approach to the study of abnormality.* In press. Seattle: Special Child Publications.

Battle, J., and Andriashek, S. 1980. The effects of partial mainstreaming on the self-esteem of special education students. Edmonton, Alberta: Edmonton Public Schools.

Battle, J., and Meston, J. 1976. The effects that camping have on self-esteem. Edmonton, Alberta: Edmonton Public Schools.

Beck., A. T., and Young, J. E. 1978. College blues. *Psychology Today* 12:80-92.

Beker, J. 1960. The influence of school camping on the self-concepts and social relationships of sixth-grade school children. *Journal of Educational Psychology* 51:352-356.

Branden, N. 1969. *The psychology of self-esteem.* Los Angeles: Nash Publishing.

Brookover, W. B.; Sailor, T.; and Paterson, A. 1965. Self-concept of ability and school achievement. *Sociology of Education* 37:271-278.

Burns, R. B. 1979. *The self-concept in theory, measurement, development, and behavior.* London: Longman.

Burns, R. B. 1982. *Self-concept development and education.* New York: Holt, Rinehart, and Winston.

Byrne, D. E. 1974. *An introduction to personality: research, theory, and applications*, 2nd ed. Englewood Cliffs, New Jersey: Prentice-Hall.

Canfield, J., and Wells, H. C. 1976. *One hundred ways to enhance self-concept in the classroom: a handbook for teachers and parents.* Englewood Cliffs, New Jersey: Prentice-Hall.

Coopersmith, S. 1962. Explorations of self-esteem. In *Child and education.* Proceedings of the 14th International Congress of Applied Psychology (Copenhagen), pp. 61-78.

Coopersmith, S. 1967. *Antecedents of self-esteem.* San Francisco: W. H. Freeman.

Dinkmeyer, D., and Dinkmeyer, D., Jr. 1982. *DUSO: Developing understanding of self and others.* Circle Pines, Minnesota: American Guidance Service.

Dinkmeyer, D., and McKay, M. 1976. *Systematic training for effective parenting: parents' handbook.* Circle Pines, Minnesota: American Guidance Service.

Dreikurs, R.; Grunwald, B. B.; and Pepper, F. C. 1971. *Maintaining sanity in the classroom.* New York: Harper.

Frager, A. J., and Stern, C. 1970. Learning by teaching. *The Reading Teacher* 23:5, pp 403-406.

Growth Associates. n.d. *Self-concept source book: ideas and activities for building self-esteem.* Rochester, New York.

Hobbs, N. 1975. *Issues in the classification of children,* vol. 1. San Francisco: Jossey-Bass.

Kashani, J.; Husain, A.; Shekim, W.O.; Hodges, K. K.; Cytryn, L.; and McKnew, D. H. 1981. Current perspectives on childhood depression: an overview. *American Journal of Psychiatry* 138:2, pp. 143-153.

Labenne, W. D., and Green, B. I. 1969. *Educational implications of self-concept theory.* Pacific Palisades, California: Goodyear Publishing.

Mettee, D. R.; Williams, A.; and Reed, H. D. 1972. Facilitating self-image enhancement and improving reading performance in young Black males. Unpublished paper. New Haven, Connecticut: Yale University.

Mehr, M., and Walker, B. A. 1983. Adolescent suicide, a family crisis: a model for effective intervention by family therapists. *Adolescence* (Summer) 18:70, pp. 285-292.

Miller, J. P. 1975. *Suicide and Adolescence* 10:37, pp. 11-24.

Mitchell, J. J. 1975. *The adolescent predicament.* Toronto: Holt, Rinehart, and Winston of Canada.

Murray, D. C. 1973. Suicidal and depressive feelings among college students. *Psychological Reports* 33:1, pp. 175-181.

Muller, D. G., and Leonetti, R. 1974. *Primary self-concept inventory.* Technical report. Austin, Texas: Learning Concepts.

Nelson, H. 1971. County suicide rate up sharply among young. *Los Angeles Times* (January 26).

Paananen, N. R. 1983. Incidence and characteristics of depression in late childhood: an exploratory study. Doctoral dissertation. Edmonton, Alberta: University of Alberta.

Pausnau, R., and Russell, A. T. 1975. Psychiatrist resident suicide: an analysis of five cases. *American Journal of Psychiatry* 132:4, pp. 402-406.

Peck, M. A., and Schrut, A. 1971. Suicidal behavior among college students. *HSMHA Reports* 86:2, pp. 149-156.

Public Law 94-142. Education for All Handicapped Children Act. Sect. 121.A.5(9).

Purkey, W. W. 1970. *Self-concept and school achievement.* Englewood Cliffs, New Jersey: Prentice-Hall.

Rogers, C. R. 1951. *Client-centered therapy: its current practice, implications, and therapy.* Boston: Houghton-Mifflin.

Rogers, C. R. 1959. A theory of therapy, personality, and interpersonal relationships as developed in a client-centered framework. In *Psychology: a study of science,* ed. Koch. New York: McGraw-Hill.

Rohn, R. D., Sartes, R. M.; Kenny, T. J.; Reynolds, B. J.; and Heald, F. P. 1977. Adolescents who attempt suicide. *Journal of Pediatrics* 90:636-638.

Rosenberg, M. 1965. *Society and adolescent self-image.* Princeton, New Jersey: Princeton University Press.

Rosenberg, M. 1979. *Conceiving the self.* New York: Basic Books.

Samuels, S. C. 1977. *Enhancing self-concept in early childhood: theory and practice.* New York: Human Science Press.

Schneidman, E. S.; Parker, E.; and Funkhouser, G. R. 1970. Youth and death. *Psychology Today* 4:3, pp. 67-72.

Schneidman, E. S., and Farberow, N. L. 1961. U.S. Govt. Printing Office PHS no. 852.

Schultz, G. A. 1983. The relationship of self-esteem and birth order: a study of grade-five children. Master's thesis. Edmonton, Alberta: University of Alberta.

Seiden, B. H. 1966. Campus tragedy: a study of student suicide. *Journal of Abnormal Psychology* 71:389-399.

Shaffer, D. 1974. Suicide in childhood and early adolescence. *Journal of Child Psychology and Psychiatry* 15: 275-291.

Simon, N. 1976. *Why am I different?* Chicago: A. Whitman.

Smith, D. M.; Dokecki, P. R.; and Davis, E. E. 1977. School-related factors influencing the self-concepts of children with learning problems. *Peabody Journal of Education* 54:185-195.

Snygg, D., and Combs, A. W. 1959. *Individual behavior.* New York: Harper and Row.

Staines, J. W. 1958. The self-picture as a factor in the classroom. *British Journal of Educational Psychology* 18: 97-111.

Stanley, E. J., and Barter, J. T. 1970. Adolescent suicidal behavior. *American Journal of Orthopsychiatry* 40:1, pp. 87-96.

Sullivan, A. M. 1974. Psychology and teaching. *Canadian Journal of Behavioral Science* (January) 6:1, pp. 1-29.

Sullivan, H. S. 1947. *Conceptions of modern psychiatry.* Washington, D.C.: William Alanson White Psychiatric Foundation.

Sullivan, H. S. 1949. The theory of anxiety and the nature of psychotherapy. *Psychiatry Quarterly* 12:3.

Thomas, J. B. 1973. *Self-concept in psychology and education: a review of research.* New York: Humanities Press.

United States Monthly Vital Statistics. 1982, vol. 31.

Wedemeyer, C. A. 1953. Gifted achievers and nonachievers. *Journal of Higher Education* 24:25-30.

Witty, P. A. 1952. Gifted children: our nation's greatest resource. *Today's Health* 12:20.

Yaniw, L. 1983. The relationship between three affective variables and student achievement. Master's thesis. Edmonton, Alberta: University of Alberta.

Yeudall, L. T. 1977. Clinical assessment system for dis-

turbed adolescents. Edmonton, Alberta: Alberta
Provincial Hospital.

Yeudall, L. T. 1977. Neuropsychological correlates of criminal psychopathology. Paper presented to the Fifth International Seminar in Comparative Clinical Criminology (Montreal).